Combustible/Burn

A Play

Andrew Silver

Mercer
University
Press
MMII

ISBN 0-86554-836-6
MUP/P238

This is a Penfield Book, an imprint of Mercer University Press.
The publication of this book is made possible in part due to a generous
subvention from the University Commons at Mercer University.

© 2002 Mercer University Press
6316 Peake Road
Macon, Georgia 31210-3960
All rights reserved

First Edition.

∞The paper used in this publication meets the
minimum requirements of American National
Standard for Infor-mation Sciences—
Permanence of Paper for Printed Library
Materials, ANSI Z39.48-1992.

Library of Congress Cataloging-in-Publication Data

Silver, Andrew.
Combustible/burn : a play / Andrew Silver.—1st ed.
p. cm.
ISBN 0-86554-836-6 (alk. paper)
1. Bryan, G. McLeod—Drama. 2. Mercer University—Drama. 3. White
college teachers—Drama. 4. Civil rights movements—Drama. 5. Civil
rights workers—Drama. 6. School integration—Drama. 7. African
Americans—Drama. 8. College students—Drama. 9. Race
relations—Drama. 10. Georgia—Drama.
I. Title.
PS3619.I545C66 2002
812'.6—dc21

2002009161

For all Mercerians who work for social justice

Mercer University Commons:
A Center for Faith and Vocation

Margaret Dee Bratcher, Dean

In October 2000, the Lilly Endowment awarded the University a grant for the Theological Exploration of Vocation. This grant affords Mercer an extraordinary opportunity to advance its educational mission and program. As a result, we are engaged throughout the University in new efforts to help students recognize life's calling and purpose, prepare for their future work in light of their faith and learning, and develop their capacities for leadership and service to church and society. Implementation of the vocation grant has centered in the establishment of University Commons as a new division in the University.

The scope of the Commons encompasses every aspect of the University. If we can accomplish the tasks before us, we will better serve the needs of our students. If we can hear again our own call to the vocation of educating men and women, we may renew the heritage of our founding as a center of faith and learning among freedom-loving Baptists. If we are successful in developing innovative programs across the disciplines and campuses, we will realize the strength of nine colleges and schools for the future of the University. *Combustible/Burn* is a significant testament to our work and vision. University Commons is proud to have supported Professor Andrew Silver in writing his play and, now, to subvent its publication.

Combustible/Burn

G. McLeod "Mac" Bryan

Sam Oni

Contents

Introduction	ix
Author's Note	xiii

Act I   1

Prologue	3
Soul Liberty	4
Liberals in Hell	7
A God Bigger Than That	8
Christian Ethics	9
Counterpoint: White School	11
Eating Standing Up	12
Counterpoint: The Back Porch	15
Bryanites	16
Brands	19
Counterpoint: Look-At Park	23
Other Mothers	23
Counterpoint: Someone Else's Kids	25
The Horse and the Mule	26
God Has a Schedule Too	27
Counterpoint: Watching My Mother Cry	29
Who is My Mother?	29
Counterpoint: An Anger Deferred	32
Koinonia	35
A Friendly, Dangerous Place	43
The Little Children of the World	43
Counterpoint: If Jesus Came Back	46
Mary and Martha	47
Silent Conspiracies	50
Remnants	54
Cookout	57
Troublemaker	65
Sweet Potato Farm	66

ACT II   71

Callings	73
Incident on Route 17	74
Hilltop Christians	77
The Land and the Gospel	80
Revelation	81
Rufus Harris	83
Missionary in Reverse	87
Do-Gooders	90
Go Back and Dream Again	91
Warm Welcome	92
Mary and Betty	98
Eleven Ways of Looking at a Black Girl	100
The Invisible	109
Papa Joe	111
Skin	114
The Mirror	116
Gospel Music Seminar	119
The Church Crucified	121
Ed Bacon's Vision	126
Closure	128

TIMELINE   133

Introduction

> "Never doubt the ability of a small group of determined citizens to change the world; indeed it's the only thing that ever has."
>
> —Margaret Mead

From 1948 to 1956, at the height of the cold war, a tight-knit group of students at a small Baptist university in Macon, Georgia helped topple segregation. Energized by a visionary professor named G. McLeod "Mac" Bryan, they stood against fellow students, parents, community, and denomination in their support of desegregation at any cost in their school, in their towns, and in their country. Their detractors called these radical students "Bryanites"—followers of Mac Bryan.

The Bryanites carried anti-Klan placards at Klan rallies, shared a common bank account from which they gave to the poor, joined in integrated house-building projects, broke segregation laws on buses and in parks, joined integrated communes, invited African Americans into their classrooms and into their homes, and preached integration in black and white churches. For their active compassion, the Bryanites found themselves disciplined, fired, jailed, and abused. Yet the work of this small group of idealistic students, along with a courageous African man and a generation of extraordinarily brave African Americans, eventually compelled their alma mater, Mercer University, to become the first private university in Georgia to desegregate. In the process, they spurred one local church to become the first Baptist congregation in Georgia to desegregate its membership. This is their story in their own words.

For Mac Byran and his students, segregation was a symptom of a deeper problem with the Baptist church as they saw it. While churches in their communities focused upon the individual's salvation in the next world, the Bryanites countered that these churches had ignored Jesus's prophetic call to communal justice and world-healing here on earth, especially for the poor and outcast. While the churches embodied a hierarchy of white men in positions of churchly authority, the Bryanites saw that they had ignored the equal fellowship of African Americans and women. For the Bryanites, the white church's refusal to address economic injustice and segregation amounted to a "conspiracy of silence" in the South. "These were all Baptist students for the most part," Mac Bryan explains, "and they were saying '*why is our denomination*—the largest, most prominent denomination—not saying a word!' That's the conspiracy of silence." The Bryanites saw themselves in a pitched battle for the spiritual heart of the Baptist denomination—a battle that, fifty years later, they still see themselves fighting.

The title of *Combustible/Burn* comes from the Bryanites' underground Christian newspaper which argued against both segregation and a legalistic interpretation of Christianity more concerned with preserving social mores and traditional authority than with working for social justice and alleviating suffering. The newspaper was so radical, mentioning the names of those who were in danger of losing their jobs or their lives in promoting integration, that students were supposed to read it and then burn it. The preservation of the individual newspaper was less important than the action readers took after reading it.

Though the group, true to the vision of the original Baptist thinkers, stood directly opposed to any creedal statements whatsoever, in a 1952 edition of "Combustible/Burn," they did provide a kind of statement of their principles. They are as follows:

> We stand for the break-down of all things that create prestige-seeking class-consciousness: secret clubs, fraternities and sororities, ostentatious behavior and possessions.
>
> We stand for a minimum standard of living based on the necessities, rather than the luxuries of life, complete

sharing, beginning in our homes, of the things we own with our brethren who sacrifice and our neighbors who need.

We stand for the free, honest, and rigorous pursuit of Truth and the exchange of ideas in a fearless forum.

We stand for the ecumenical fellowship of Christians as over against narrow creeds and a self-centered concern for institutional denominations.

We stand for alternatives to war, iron-curtain propaganda, nationalistic patriotism, and armaments: this may be the path of all-out pacifism or lesser degrees of variation upon that.

We stand for the complete integration of all people, with equal opportunities beginning in our homes and for every new-born child.

We stand for the sense of Christian vocation in its deepest and widest implications.

We will accept each person for what he—or she—is.

Later, Sam Oni—the African student who eventually desegregated Mercer University—spoke of a similar notion of Christian justice: "There's a kind of naturalness and liberation in recognizing the divine in yourself and others," Sam explained. "Once you recognize the divine in you and in me, and you behave consistent with that knowledge, you're liberated; you're brother's liberated; your sister's liberated; and then that becomes a dance."

Here in the twenty-first century, more than fifty years after the Bryanites began to challenge segregation, we have yet to accept our invitations to this dance.

Though a considerable part of this project involves the act of witnessing to past suffering, most of my interview subjects would be saddened at the prospect of this play being read or viewed as a history play about an American triumph over injustices that no longer exist, or that exist today in a much lesser form. Most of those interviewed believe that the civil rights era failed to achieve its goals, and that the institutional church has grown yet less concerned with social injustice than it was in the fifties. As Mac put it: "we lost the battle for genuine integration."

A glance at the recent history of racial inequity in this country will tell us that most cities are still segregated in America, and that the North has managed to outpace the South in the extent of its segregation. A glance at our education system will tell us that public education in America is as inequitable as it ever was and still starkly segregated. In the South, the limited advances in educational integration since the early seventies have been reversed in the last decade, and we find our schools resegregated once more.

Though my interview subjects told me of their disappointment in our limited progress over the last fifty years, they remain characteristically hopeful for a change to come with a new generation of activists against injustice both here at home and abroad. Furman York told me, "Mac Bryan and his group were few, but they accomplished a lot. The people he affected made a great change…and that's what you all need to do."

I'd like to dedicate this play to Mercer faculty, staff and students, but especially the "remnant" in every generation of students everywhere that, in the face of opposition from family and friends, fights against discrimination in the church and in the state, and against all forms of violence, with undying love and compassion. You represent the prophetic calling yet burning. You are this century's heroes.

Andrew Silver
Macon, Georgia
2002

Author's Note

The seeds of this theater project were planted by Anna Deveare Smith, a playwright whose plays about communities in conflict—fashioned from interview excerpts with people in those communities—helped shape what is now called "documentary theater." Unlike "realistic" theater, documentary theater is constructed by weaving together the actual voices of living people and historical documents, focusing not on a traditional plot ("who gets the girl?"), but on a specific theme ("what does it *mean* to be a girl in Georgia?"). Action and even character are less important in these plays than voices and perspectives; watching is less important than listening and responding. Rather than the playwright imagining characters from different cultural backgrounds in isolation, the playwright works with a community to essentially co-author a play. What I love about Smith's plays is the way in which theater becomes local again: the product of a community with the potential to open up avenues of communication and discovery within that community.

From the first, this has been a project defined in collaboration with community, colleagues and students. Last June, with the support of the Lilly Endowment, I assembled a group of three talented students to help interview a total of 120 people active in the early civil rights movement and then transcribe nearly three hundred hours worth of interviews for this project. Almost every word of this play comes directly from roughly fifty of these interviews and the research conducted in Jack Tarver's special collections. The members of the group were as follows:

Eme Crawford: Director of Research
Angela Parris: Research Assistant
Jessica Smith: Research Assistant

Our group met throughout the summer with Professor Paul Oppy, the director (and my good friend and constant counsel), to share our transcripts, to shape a vision of what this play ought to be about, and to experiment with broad sections of what is now the text of *Combustible/Burn*. After we finished interviewing, we began assembling groups to read very rough drafts of the play—essentially various patterns of the transcripts. The script changed along the way in significant ways due to astute critiques offered by, among others, Amanda Voss, Bethany Rezek, Jessica Smith, Jennifer Baldwin, Natalie Moss, Pamela Patterson, Nathan Poling, Emily Barringer, Lauren Hauser, Paul Oppy, and especially Eme Crawford, whose tireless work and input on this project was invaluable. Sam Oni, a frequent visitor to our workshops, provided inspiration to me and the cast throughout, his warmth and generosity of spirit positively addictive. Thanks also to Will Campbell, an indefatigable voice for social justice himself for the last half-century, whose *Stem of Jesse* first introduced me to this story.

Dr. Anya Krugovoy Silver, my wife and colleague in the English Department, deserves special thanks not only for helping shape the play and reading countless revisions, but also for her sustaining support and humor during the process of writing the play. Special thanks too to Tom Glennon, Tom Huber, and especially Dee Bratcher, all of whom offered unstinting encouragement and the resources of the Lilly Foundation, assistance which helped bring *Combustible/Burn* to fruition. The cast for the premiere—Emily Barringer, Cara Gibson, Lauren Hauser, Julie Jones, Kim Kight, Pamela Patterson, Patrick Sinclair, Jim Sisson, Tim Smith, and Charles Thomas—was an inspiration under the fine direction of Paul Oppy, helping shape the play in innumerable ways. They are family now: a beautiful example of the beloved community that Sam Oni, Mac Bryan and Joe Hendricks had envisioned for Mercer's campus. Thanks finally to President Kirby Godsey, whose progressive leadership helped inspire this play and whose protection of Mercer's freedom of inquiry made the play possible.

Of course, this play would not have been possible in the first place had it not been for the voices of people who shared their stories and their often painful memories with me and the project. It took courage to break the silence then and it takes courage to once again break the silence and relive painful memories today. Listening to these beautiful, generous people—none of whom have forgotten their callings—was a joy and a humbling, learning experience for me. I hope against hope that I have done some justice to their stories and their lives.

One more note: since the text of this play comes from the spoken memories of those who lived through desegregation, it carries all of the subjective biases of individual recollections. Together, they speak a truth that can only be experienced and spoken of subjectively.

CHARACTERS

Actor 1: Mac Bryan, Don Baxter, Harold McManus, Rufus Harris, Clarence Jordan and other narrators and students.

Actor 2: Clifford York, Joe Hendricks, Johnny Mitchell, Walter Moore and other narrators, students and Koinonians.

Actor 3: Harris Mobley, Furman York, Ed Bacon, Bob Otto and other narrators, students and Koinonians.

Actor 4: Nancy Attaway, Amelia Barclay, Mrs. McGuinness, White Teacher and other narrators, students and Koinonians.

Actor 5: Jan York, Lawrence Hardy, Betty Friedan, and other narrators, students and Koinonians.

Actor 6: Carolyn Martin, Mary Wilder and other narrators, students, and Koinonians.

Actor 7: Betty J. Walker, Ernestine Cole, Young Samaria "Cookie" Mitchum, Thelma Dillard, Catherine Meeks and other narrators, students and Koinonians.

Actor 8: Samaria "Cookie" Mitchum, Palmira Braswell and other narrators, students and Koinonians.

Actor 9: Sam Oni, Gary Johnson, Mark Glover, Mayor C. Jack Ellis, Alma Jackson, Richard Scott, John and other narrators, students and Koinonians.

Actor 10: Rev. Lonzy Edwards, Carl Byas, Bus-rider, God, teenage Samaria "Cookie" Mitchum, Lydia Dumas, and other narrators, students and Koinonians.

"Bryanites"

Clifford York

Jan York

Nancy Attaway

Einar Michaelson

The Bryanites and Georgia Baptist Junior College students painting buildings together in 1950

Carolyn Martin as a bride

White children playing in the fountains at a segregated Washington Park

Koinonia children, including Carolyn Martin's daughters, in front of the integrated farm

Harris Mobley

Harris Mobley eating fried fufu and peanut soup with Pastors S.O Akinleye and I.O Hmood in Ghana

Sam Oni's freshman photo

Don Baxter as a center for the Mercer Bears

Mary Wilder

Rufus Harris

Samaria "Cookie" Mitcham graduating with honors from an integrated Miller High School

Ed Bacon

Gary Johnson

Ernestine P. Cole

Act I

"The question is not whether we will be extremist but what kind of extremist will we be. Will we be extremists for hate or will we be extremists for love?"

—Martin Luther King, Jr.,
"Letter from a Birmingham Jail"

Joe Hendricks

Prologue

ACTOR 8/NARRATOR: *From the Atlanta Constitution:*

ACTOR 10/NARRATOR: On the bright fall morning of Sunday, September 25, 1966, Sam Oni, then a senior at Mercer University—

ACTOR 7/NARRATOR: who three years ago became Mercer's first Negro student—

ACTOR 10/NARRATOR: presented himself at Tattnall Square Baptist Church.

ACTOR 8/NARRATOR: He was stopped by ushers who blocked his way.

ACTOR 9/SAM ONI: I told them how God's house should be open to God's children.

ACTOR 7/NARRATOR: When Oni insisted that he be admitted, he was seized by two men of the church.

ACTOR 10/NARRATOR: One applied a headlock on him and the other dragged him down the steps.

ACTOR 8/NARRATOR: The church had voted 286 to 109 last summer to remain segregated.

ACTOR 2/NARRATOR: Combustible—

ACTOR 7/NARRATOR: Combustible—

ACTOR 10/NARRATOR: Combustible—

ACTOR 6/NARRATOR: Combustible—

ACTOR 9/NARRATOR *(soft)*: Burn.

Soul Liberty

ACTOR 1/HAROLD MCMANUS *(Professor of Christianity, Mercer University, 1948-1985. In a soft-spoken and deliberate North Carolinian accent)*: The Baptist faith was originally simply an expression, or outburst, of what our founders spoke of as soul—s-o-u-l—liberty.

ACTOR 6/FIRST BAPTIST *(patronizing)*: Soul liberty.

ACTOR 5/SECOND BAPTIST *(somber)*: Soul liberty.

ACTOR 2/THIRD BAPTIST *(dogmatic)*: Soul liberty.

ACTOR 3/RADICAL BAPTIST *(jumping up, shouting, and dancing wildly)*: Soul liberty!!

(ACTORS 6, 5, AND 2 *stare disapprovingly at* ACTOR 3, ACTOR 2 *claps twice, a group of actors quickly mime gagging* ACTOR 3, *and in a moment drag him into a jail space upstage left. All look up contentedly and smile at the audience in unison. Together, in a tightly controlled voice.)*

ACTORS 2, 5, AND 6: Soul liberty.

ACTOR 1/HAROLD MCMANUS: Soul liberty. Freedom. The privilege of interpreting scriptures for ourselves under the guidance of the holy spirit, which begot the idea that each person is his or her own priest, as it were, before God. You don't need the intermediary efforts of church or clergy. We *never* had creedal statements. Never. And a blank line, "now sign right here." That's *so* un-Baptist! Freedom of scriptural interpretation. Always. And that has been both a blessing and a bane in Baptist life especially. For when we were fighting some of the battles in the fifties with local preachers or with denominational leaders and so on, each side would claim—

ACTOR 6/FIRST BAPTIST: "Well, I'm just following my own conscience here."

ACTOR 1/HAROLD MCMANUS (*Chuckling*): You know—

ACTOR 2/THIRD BAPTIST: "This is the way I read the bible."

ACTOR 1/HAROLD MCMANUS: And there's hardly any comeback to that, once you "announce" that's where you stand. So, it was rough. But uh, it was again, just soul liberty. S-o-u-l. Soul liberty. Freedom.

ACTOR 8/NARRATOR: From Macon newspapers, letters and sermons, 1950-1963:

(*Read in convincing, self-assured, warm voices.*)

ACTOR 2/SEGREGATIONIST: Dear Christian Believers. We believe it a crime directed at God to advocate integration or support it and not speak up for segregation—

ACTOR 6/SEGREGATIONIST: The basic requirement God set up for his "holy" people was racial segregation—

ACTOR 4/SEGREGATIONIST: Deuteronomy 7:3—

ACTOR 3/SEGREGATIONIST: "Thou art an holy people. Neither shall thou make marriages with them; thy daughter thou shalt not give unto his son, nor his daughter shalt thou take unto thy son."

ACTOR 5/SEGREGATIONIST: It is evident God's wish was separation of the races.

ACTOR 3/SEGREGATIONIST: Acts 17:26—

ACTOR 6/SEGREGATIONIST: "God hath made of one blood all nations of men for to dwell on all the face of the earth, and hath determined the *bounds* of their habitation."

ACTOR 4/SEGREGATIONIST: It is only when certain members of the one race or the other have tried to step out of the bounds of their own habitations that they had trouble.

ACTOR 3/SEGREGATIONIST: Jesus taught inequality among men. Jesus taught discerning love. Racial segregation as a social organization fits that pattern.

ACTOR 5/SEGREGATIONIST: Save our churches and our country from communist inspired integration.

ACTOR 2/SEGREGATIONIST: You may as a segregationist know, that what your experience, instinct, and intellect have told you is right in race relations—

ACTORS 2, 3, 4, 5, 6: is also Christian—

ACTOR 6/SEGREGATIONIST *(smiling)*: If you agree with these principles, please sign and forward to your pastor.

LIBERALS IN HELL

ACTOR 3/BOB OTTO *(Mercer Chaplain and Professor of Christianity, 1956-1988. He speaks in a rich, slow, open, midwestern accent)*: I must have inherited a kind of intellectual interest in things. Questions interested me. And it never occurred to me that I was wrong in raising questions. I remember when I was a sophomore at this very conservative school a freshman student coming up to me and saying:

(A FRESHMAN STUDENT walks up to YOUNG OTTO, both carrying books.)

ACTOR 4/FRESHMAN STUDENT *(sanctimonious)*: I just wanted to tell you that I belong to a small prayer group, and we pray for you every week.

ACTOR 3/BOB OTTO: And I said—

ACTOR 2/YOUNG OTTO: Well, why are you praying for me?

ACTOR 4/FRESHMAN STUDENT: Well, you are asking questions that shouldn't be asked and you are saying things that shouldn't be said.

ACTOR 3/BOB OTTO: I was not aware of that. Somebody else was. *(laughs)* And it became clear to me in my first year in the seminary that I really *was* asking questions, and I was thinking thoughts, that were out of the mainstream of fundamentalism. And I remember *really* being agitated by this, because at *that* time, in that kind of conservative environment and fundamentalist environment, liberals were people who were damned and going to hell. *(beat)* And I seemed to be moving in that direction. So I thought I was going to go to hell. I think only a fundamentalist can appreciate the agony that that creates, you know. I remember going to bed one night, praying to God, something like this:

ACTOR 2/YOUNG OTTO *(praying, head bowed)*: Dear God, I think I'm becoming a liberal. And if I do that means I'll go to hell. So I'd rather die tonight and go to heaven and be with you, than to go on living. . . and become a real liberal. . . and go to hell.

ACTOR 3/BOB OTTO: Now, do you feel the agony in that? Ah, but I've often used the illustration that once you start thinking critically, it's like getting on a ski-jump: once you start down on your skis, you can't stop in the middle! Once you start thinking and raising questions, looking at things in different ways, you *can't* stop. There's *nothing* that's going to stop you!

(YOUNG OTTO puts on a tie and becomes CLIFFORD YORK.)

A God Bigger Than That

ACTOR 2/CLIFFORD YORK *(Mercer class of 1954, speaks in a taut voice with a slight North Georgia mountain accent)*: My father was a lay Baptist minister in Needy Creek. And he got someone from Atlanta who provided them with a tent and he started a church. It was extremely conservative fundamentalist Baptist. You know, the Presbyterians I remember, the Catholics—there were no Catholic churches, but they had *heard* of Catholics—and uh, they were damned to hell. You know, everybody except the Baptists who thought as they did. And I remember one of my big insights, if I've had any, is when I was in high school, and I would hear them talking about how the Methodists, no matter how well intended they were, and the Presbyterians there in Clayton, they were all going to hell. And I remember being shocked at myself because

I thought—I was maybe fifteen—"I can think of a God bigger than that."

ACTOR 5: I can think of a God—

ACTOR 7: I can think of a God—

ACTOR 3: I can think of a God—

ACTOR 10: I can think of a God—

ACTORS 3, 5, 7, 2, 10: Bigger than that.

ACTOR 2/CLIFFORD YORK: That was very disturbing to me. That's when my life opened up and I started questioning things. And when I got to Mercer, the atmosphere was just perfect for me to just revel in this new world. That's where I met Mac Bryan.

CHRISTIAN ETHICS

(Actors 1-6 become students entering a classroom.)

ACTOR 5/STUDENT: G. Macleoud Bryan—

ACTOR 6/STUDENT: Tall and thin—

ACTOR 3/STUDENT: Real skinny—

ACTOR 4/STUDENT: He's always been just a shadow.

ACTOR 2/STUDENT: He was a gangly guy—big Adam's apple—he was the Ichabod Crane of Mercer.

ACTOR 5/STUDENT: Wild haired, wild-eyed—

ACTOR 6/STUDENT: We called him:

ACTORS 2-6: Mac.

(They sit as if in a classroom. Lights up on MAC BRYAN, Mercer professor of Christianity, 1948-1956. He is animated, unkempt, charismatic, tall and wiry. He has an intuitive sense of the theatrical and modulates his voice accordingly, but the gravelly whisper is his favorite mode of speaking. He speaks quickly, urgently, and with a smile. Whenever MAC says "see" or "that sorta thing," it is always barely heard, as a kind of whispered punctuation. His students say he derives therapy from opposition: this utter joy in the face of danger should be apparent throughout.)

ACTOR 3/STUDENT: Mac taught Christian ethics at Mercer University in the forties and fifties. *(laughs)* He was forever debunking the sacred cows of cracker society.

ACTOR 4/STUDENT: We had one white boy in our Christian Ethics class who was in a wheel chair and there was a young black man who pushed him from class to class.

(ACTOR 9, stage left, appears as the African American man waiting outside the class.)

And he wasn't allowed to come into our classroom. He'd have to wait out in the hall while we had our Christian Ethics class—

ACTOR 1/MAC BRYAN: —and he was a bright fellow, and I could see that he had a lot of intellectual curiosity. And I would get to talking with him in the hall and the students were coming in before class—and he was not able to go to college. And so I simply said to him one day "look, it's ridiculous for you to stand out in the hall when there's plenty of room in the classroom and all you have to do is come in and just be a part of the class."

ACTOR 6/STUDENT: And we put it to a vote in the class.

(The class raises their hands.)

ACTOR 4/STUDENT: And we voted that the young black man, who had to go out into the hall and stand, should stay in our class and learn something, rather than have to go out and stand in the hallway.

(ACTOR 9 enters and awkwardly takes a seat among the white students.)

ACTOR 1/MAC BRYAN: Well, it didn't take twenty-four hours for that to get back to the administration.

ACTOR 2/STUDENT: And at the end of the evening, Dr. Bryan was notified that there were calls coming in from trustees and others around the state that that could not be tolerated.

(ACTOR 9 silently gets up and moves back to the edge of the stage, head down.)

ACTOR 1/MAC BRYAN: And that was immediately tabooed. They didn't say a thing to me. They said to the student: "You don't go back in that classroom again." So *he's* the victim.

COUNTERPOINT: WHITE SCHOOL

ACTOR 7/BETTY J WALKER *(Maconite and Mercer class of 1968)*: My friends and I would cut across Mercer's campus to get to football games. And I remember seeing Mercer's campus when I was a kid. I saw the quad, and everything looked so clean and beautiful and such. And I thought "this is the college that I'm going to go to." I didn't know the name of the college, but on the way back I saw that it was Mercer University. And I said to myself, "I'll go to Mercer University." When I got home my mother said "get that out of your head, you are a black child and that is a white school."

(*Pause.*)

And I felt crushed by that.

EATING STANDING UP

ACTOR 6/STUDENT: So that was the world of Mercer that we knew, and it was the world of "separate but equal."

ACTOR 4/STUDENT: Mac had students come over to his house once or twice a week in the evenings to talk about social injustices and segregation—

ACTOR 1/MAC BRYAN: So every Wednesday night, see, we'd have these meetings, and I'd usually try to bring in people from all over the world. So on this particular night, two black missionaries from the Southern Baptist missionary society came to the house. I said, "Come on in, sit down until the students come." Ok, the students came, and my wife fixed supper for this crowd. And for most of these students it was the first time they ever ate socializing as equals with blacks. Well the students had gone home, and before midnight the phone rang. And Mercer University's President is on the other line. Of course that never happens.

(*Picks up, then covers the receiver. To the audience.*)

If the president of Mercer were to call you at midnight, you'd know something was up.

(ACTOR 3, as PRESIDENT, is concerned, avuncular. There is nothing unreasonable in his tone.)

ACTOR 3/PRESIDENT: Mac, I heard you had a Negro at the house.

ACTOR 1/MAC BRYAN: That's what he said, "Mac I heard you had a Negro." I said "Yes, Mr. President, certainly did. What's the problem?" He said —

ACTOR 3/PRESIDENT: Well, I had trustees calling me, and they want to know what I'm going to do about it.

ACTOR 1/MAC BRYAN: See. I mean, see, the President was under pressure constantly about, you know, this kind of behavior from some conservative power structure. I said "Mr. President," I said, "would you, if two Southern Baptist Missionaries come by your house, and they didn't have a place to have supper, would you feed 'em?"

ACTOR 3/PRESIDENT *(impatient)*: Did you feed them?

ACTOR 1/MAC BRYAN: Yes, we fed them. We have a group of students in every Wednesday night. We eat together.

ACTOR 3/PRESIDENT: You had students?

ACTOR 1/MAC BRYAN: Yes, we had students.

ACTOR 3/PRESIDENT: Well that's I think how the trustees found out about it. One of the trustee's daughters was in the group.

(Lights up on TRUSTEE'S DAUGHTER *sitting next to* TRUSTEE, *with opera glasses.)*

ACTOR 1/MAC BRYAN *(to the audience)*: She left early and went to a music concert as I found out, and she blurted out to her uncle that you know—

ACTOR 4/TRUSTEE'S DAUGHTER *(seated, turning to her father as if she can no longer contain herself)*: I just had the greatest experience in my life! I ate with a *Negro*!

(The TRUSTEE, *aghast, drops his opera glasses.)*

ACTOR 1/MAC BRYAN: And ah, of course, he said—

ACTOR 2/TRUSTEE: That was the worst thing that ever happened to you, young lady, and I'm going to see if I can stop it.

ACTOR 1/MAC BRYAN: See. So, things like that began working immediately. I mean that's how fast it worked. From, you know, five o'clock till twelve o'clock. And the President's caught in the middle of that.

ACTOR 3/PRESIDENT: How did you feed them all?

ACTOR 1/MAC BRYAN: Well, my wife fixed the meal and people bring in meals—

ACTOR 3/PRESIDENT *(louder, interrupting him, excited by something)*: Did you sit down?

ACTOR 1/MAC BRYAN: Nope—

ACTOR 3/PRESIDENT *(louder, suddenly pleased)*: You didn't sit down?

ACTOR 1/MAC BRYAN: Nope, we—we don't have enough room for people to sit down—

ACTOR 3/PRESIDENT *(cutting him off)*: That's all I needed to know.

ACTOR 1/MAC BRYAN: And he hung up. Now, notice, he didn't defend me. Not the least bit. All he did was he took the oldest Southern defense that you do not eat sitting down with the black. If it just so happens that you're standing up and the black's standing up and eating with you, that's a happenstance. And he argued to the trustees. I didn't call that a defense at all.

COUNTERPOINT: THE BACK PORCH

ACTOR 9/MAYOR C. JACK ELLIS *(First African American Mayor of Macon, Georgia. In his bustling office after his recent election. He has a gentle voice.)*: I had a playmate who happened to be white. And I guess this was preschool, so I was four or five years old or so. And we were playing during the daytime. And I remember his mother telling us we had to come in and have lunch. And he, of course, invited me along. And I remember his mother directing me to the back porch. I didn't know why at the time—and I was wondering in my own little mind why we were playing together and doing all of the things we did together, but when it was time to have lunch, he went inside and I went to the back porch.

(Pause.)

You know, the craziest thing in the world—I could not eat at the table of my young friend, yet the same lady had a black woman in her kitchen cooking her food. Now, think about that: if you are that against having people of color in your midst, yet you trust them well enough to prepare your food. So, what are you afraid of?

BRYANITES

ACTOR 5/STUDENT: Mac knew there was a sickness in our society, and, like Martin Luther King, he did not advocate any violence whatsoever, but he advocated that people start changing things.

ACTOR 2/STUDENT: *Action!*

ACTOR 1/MAC BRYAN: We met every Wednesday night, we went to conferences, we went to Morehouse—

ACTORS 2-3/STUDENTS: *Justice!*

ACTOR 1/MAC BRYAN: We went to Koinonia—we were just going everywhere!

ACTORS 2-4/STUDENTS: *Real world!*

ACTOR 1/MAC BRYAN: It was an extra university, it was a university that didn't have courses or grades!

ACTORS 2-5/STUDENTS: *Labor!*

ACTOR 1/MAC BRYAN: We had our own bank account; we shared with people in need.

ACTORS 2-6/STUDENTS: *Desegregation!*

ACTOR 1/MAC BRYAN: We were living on the edge. They called my students—

ACTORS 7-10 *(from off-stage, ridiculing)*: "Bryanites."

ACTOR 1/MAC BRYAN: —which was a slur, meaning, you know, students who were far off on a tangent.

ACTOR 6/STUDENT: That's what the law school students called us—

ACTOR 3/STUDENT: I remember one time in the early fifties, we all went to the City Auditorium in Macon where the Klan was having a rally—

ACTOR 4/STUDENT: Mac had duplicated a bunch of handbills for us to give out, and so we went downtown—

ACTOR 3/STUDENT: —and started hanging these handbills that contradicted what the Klan said with the New Testament.

ACTOR 6/STUDENT: And we got stopped by the police. *(laughs)*

ACTOR 5/STUDENT: They said that handbills were not allowed—which you know, was a bunch of bull—

ACTOR 2/STUDENT: So we took some placards saying, "Down with the Klan!"

ACTOR 3/STUDENT: We went into the balcony of the City Auditorium and held placards against the Klan being unChristian—

ACTOR 4/STUDENT *(scribbling furiously in a small pad)*: I posed as a reporter and snuck into the Auditorium. I saw things in there that I wouldn't have *believed* if I hadn't seen it: you know, the Klan preaching—claiming biblical meaning into everything they did—

ACTOR 6/STUDENT: You know, that it was all the way God wanted it to be—the terrible way they used the scriptures to prove what they believed.

ACTOR 4/STUDENT: Some of them were the big muckety-mucks who were making speeches: they'd say that they were a Deacon in such and such a Baptist church—

ACTOR 3/STUDENT: And one of the Klansmen looked up at us and said—

(ACTOR 1, in a Klan hood, pointing his finger at the group.)

ACTOR 1/KLANSMAN: I don't blame you young men and women. It's those liberal professors at Mercer that got you thinkin' this way!

ACTOR 4/STUDENT: *That* was eye-opening.

ACTOR 2/STUDENT: The Bryanites had a newsletter called "Combustible/Burn."

ACTOR 5/STUDENT: Combustible slash burn.

ACTOR 6/STUDENT: Mac paid me to type up and edit and send out the little newspaper—

ACTOR 3/STUDENT: It was dealing with social issues—

ACTOR 6/STUDENT: —and a lot of that was about racial issues—

ACTOR 2/STUDENT: —and about religion—

ACTOR 4/STUDENT: It was so radical, you're supposed to read it and burn it.

ACTOR 6/STUDENT: And it was supposed to be burned after we read it to keep everybody out of trouble.

ACTOR 2/STUDENT: I mean, there were names there, and someone had just been fired from their church for preaching integration, and so-and-so is helping them.

ACTOR 5/STUDENT: It was an underground movement that he had with his students.

ACTOR 3/STUDENT: We had a little mini-revolution going back in the early fifties at Mercer.

Brands

ACTOR 6/STUDENT: From *Combustible/Burn*,

ACTOR 2/STUDENT: First principle: "We stand for the break-down—

ACTOR 5/STUDENT: break-down—

ACTOR 4/STUDENT: of all things that create prestige-seeking—

ACTOR 3/STUDENT: class-consciousness:

ACTOR 2/STUDENT: secret clubs—

ACTOR 5/STUDENT: fraternities and sororities—

ACTOR 4/STUDENT: ostentatious behavior—

ACTOR 6/STUDENT: and possessions."

ACTOR 4/STUDENT: Class.

ACTOR 1/MAC BRYAN: This is a Jesus story: a man lived in a rich house with a gate and a dog, and there was a poor man at the gate eating the crumbs off his table. When they died, the rich man went to hell, poor man went to the bosom of Abraham. And the rich man in hell prays to God—

ACTOR 3/RICH MAN: Please send a prophet to my rich brothers who are going to end up in hell like I am if they don't have somebody to tell them.

ACTOR 1/MAC BRYAN: And Jesus says that God said:

ACTOR 10/GOD: There's a chasm fixed between you and me that no person can cross. I have already sent prophets to your brothers and to you, and you would not listen.

ACTOR 1/MAC BRYAN: I was preaching this in Macon, Georgia in a mill church and a man came up to me at the end of the service, he said: "Preacher do I understand you to say that the poor man went to heaven just because he was poor and the rich man went to hell because he was rich?" *(smiling)* I said "I didn't make up the story, sir."

ACTOR 4/STUDENT: Bryanites:

ACTOR 2/STUDENT: I grew up in a little town called Oliver, Georgia—

ACTOR 5/STUDENT: I grew up in Statesboro, Georgia—

ACTOR 3/STUDENT: I was born in Cedartown, Georgia—

ACTOR 4/STUDENT: The Bethany community near Savannah—

ACTOR 2/STUDENT: Between Ellijay and Chatsworth: Fort Mountain, Mountain town—

ACTOR 6/STUDENT: The Appalachian mountains of North Georgia—

ACTOR 3/STUDENT: Talbotton—

ACTOR 5/STUDENT: Griffin—

ACTOR 6/STUDENT: Gainesville—

ACTOR 4/STUDENT: Albany—

ACTOR 3/STUDENT: A Georgia boy—

ACTOR 6/STUDENT: A typical Southern Baptist Georgia girl—

ACTOR 2/STUDENT: My parents were quite poor—

ACTOR 5/STUDENT: Our houses were working class houses—

ACTOR 3/STUDENT: In a poor town—

ACTOR 4/STUDENT: In the 1930's—

ACTOR 2/STUDENT: My father was a tenant farmer—

ACTOR 6/STUDENT: Mother took in sewing, and later, when I was eleven, worked in a parachute plant—

ACTOR 4/STUDENT: Both my parents worked—one in a hosiery shop and the other in Crompton Highland Corduroy, making corduroy and velvet.

ACTOR 2/STUDENT: For poor wages—

ACTOR 3/STUDENT: It was the kind of job that I would not want.

ACTOR 4/STUDENT: My sense of injustice came from the mills.

ACTOR 3/STUDENT: I saw the world through the eyes—

ACTORS 2/STUDENT: —of the underclass.

ACTOR 5/JAN YORK (*Mercer class of 1954*): We lived in what was called the mill village. I was a mill girl. And, you know, all the houses were alike. We lived practically just in front of the mill—half a block away, in the shadow of the thing.
    And there was a great distinction in those days between the mill people and the town people. And that was something that sort of stayed with me all through the years. We were considered lower than the town people.
    When I was about five or six years old, I took dancing lessons with some girls from town, and ah, they—my mother took me over to their house one day to play. In town. (*actors 6 & 4 appear as YOUNG GIRLS, whispering to themselves*) And (*laughs*) as we were playing they suggested—

ACTOR 6/A YOUNG GIRL (*giggling*): *You* play the maid and *we'll* play the ladies of the house.

(*The girls give her an apron and giggle.*)

ACTOR 5/JAN YORK: And so... I got the message. (*Pause*) You don't want to know how I felt.

(*Pause.*)

I felt terrible... it was—it was a—like a—a—a—a—... a brand. You know? You could hear the sizzle.

Counterpoint: Look-at Park

ACTOR 8/PALMIRA BRASWELL *(Macon resident and Macon's first African American woman DJ)*: Let me tell you what, what really brings it home to me: the Washington Park across from the Washington Memorial Library. The fountains are still there. In the Spring and in the Summer, the fountains would just be so beautiful. And the little white kids would be paddling in the water, the little wading pool at the fountain. And I could remember standing there looking at that park—not being able to wade in the water with the beautiful fountains. Or walk on the grass—the greenest grass I'd ever seen in my life. And I couldn't do that. It was a "look-at" park, but "do not try and wade in the water."

That park was a little piece of heaven that I could not enter. And it was because I was black.

(Pause.)

And that's—that's a childhood memory of mine.

Other Mothers

ACTOR 1/MAC BRYAN: Let me give you my definition of how people arrive at justice: once you've been treated unjustly, you cry to heaven. (*raises his fists to God, addressing the heavens*) You cry to the, to the, to the empty spaces (*intense whisper*): "Where O where is there an answer?"
That's when the sense of justice is born.
I say that's where God's born.

ACTOR 2/STUDENT: *Combustible/Burn,* second principle:

ACTOR 5/STUDENT: "We stand for the complete integration of all people—

ACTOR 3/STUDENT: Complete integration—

ACTOR 4/STUDENT: with equal opportunities beginning in our homes

ACTOR 2/STUDENT: and for every new-born child."

ACTOR 5/STUDENT: Our homes.

ACTOR 3/STUDENT: My mother died when I was six months old and a black nanny took care of me—

ACTOR 6/STUDENT: I had, I guess you'd call it a nanny nowadays—

ACTOR 2/STUDENT: Her name was Bessie Redding—

ACTOR 4/STUDENT: Her name was Polly Benfield—

ACTOR 3/STUDENT: Carrie Johnson—

ACTOR 5/STUDENT: Annie Blunt—

ACTOR 6/STUDENT: Hazel Brentson—

ACTORS 2-6/STUDENTS: She raised me—

ACTOR 4/STUDENT: And she was—she was almost as important as my mother, because she—

ACTORS 2-6/STUDENTS: She *raised* me.

ACTOR 2/STUDENT: She took care of me, she taught me manners—

ACTOR 5/STUDENT: If I had to pick somebody to be with I'd be with her—

ACTOR 3/STUDENT: She made a very profound impression on me as a child—

ACTOR 6/STUDENT: One of my favorite people in all the world—

ACTOR 4/STUDENT: And I absolutely loved her—

ACTOR 2/STUDENT: I loved her deeply.

ACTOR 4/STUDENT: Even at the age of four, I realized that she didn't sit at the table with the rest of the family when she sat—

ACTOR 5/STUDENT: And I asked the folks to let her eat with us—

ACTOR 4/STUDENT: I remember asking my mother about that—

ACTOR 5/STUDENT: And they said—

ACTORS 4 &5/STUDENTS: "No, she would not be comfortable."

ACTOR 4/STUDENT: That was the kind of answer I got. But from that moment on I didn't believe that that was justice, because I loved her so much and she was very important in my life.

Counterpoint: Someone Else's Kids

(GARY JOHNSON, Mercer class of 1970 and, later, first full-time African American professor at Mercer. In his home, over a breakfast phone call at 5 a.m., before work.)

ACTOR 9/GARY JOHNSON: My mother did work as a maid for quite awhile, maybe ten years. She hated it. She would say that being a maid was really a question of survival. I don't think she liked the idea that that other people didn't see her as a human being.

Ahh *(transformed into a sigh)*... you know, this is weird, I don't know why it sticks to my mind, but she said the one thing she hated was washing other women's underwear. Because they would just simply leave them on the floor. She thought that was particularly degrading for some reason. She would have to go around the house picking up underwear to wash.

And one day she quit. I think I was in college then, and she asked for a day off to go carry me to school and her um. . . person that she worked for told her:

ACTOR 4/WHITE WOMAN *(to the audience, as if they're her maids)*: No, you've got to iron my dresses and get dinner ready for the guests.

ACTOR 9/GARY JOHNSON: My mother said to me, "here I am taking care of someone else's kids, and I have latch-key kids." And my mother said "well this is a defining moment in my son's life and so I'm going." And I think when that hit her, she just basically walked away.

THE HORSE AND THE MULE

ACTOR 5/LAWRENCE HARDY *(Mercer class of 1952):* I remember we had an African American maid. *(Lights up on Actor 8, washing laundry in a tub)* And she gave me my first clue of the injustice. I was just about five years old. She said:

ACTOR 8/MAID *(still washing)*: Mr. Lawrence do you see the mule out there doing all the work, plowing the cornfields?

ACTOR 5/LAWRENCE HARDY: Yes, ma'am.

ACTOR 8/MAID: You see the horse over there out in the field grazing the flowers and grass?

ACTOR 5/LAWRENCE HARDY: Yes ma'am.

ACTOR 8/MAID (*stops washing, looks at LAWRENCE*): Well the horse is you white folks. And the mule is us black folks. And we do all the work, and you get all the money.

ACTOR 5/LAWRENCE HARDY: And that's the first time that I realized the inequality of it all.

God Has A Schedule Too

(*Chairs are arranged in two rows to indicate the body of a bus. White actors, including the bus- driver, are seated in front; African American actors—and LAWRENCE—are seated in the back.*)

ACTOR 1/MAC BRYAN: So Lawrence worked with black students in town—

ACTOR 5/LAWRENCE HARDY (*proudly*): My Royal Ambassadors—

ACTOR 1/MAC BRYAN: And the buses of course were segregated. And he ran immediately into segregated town, because when he went on with his black students in the black youth group, he would sit with the black students where they sat. And the bus-driver would raise hell.

ACTOR 5/LAWRENCE HARDY: Said I didn't belong back there. I had to come and sit up front with the white people.

ACTOR 2/BUS-DRIVER (*looking in the rear-view mirror*): Mister, if you're going to ride this bus, you'll have to move to the front seats.

ACTOR 5/LAWRENCE HARDY: "I'm with these students as one of them," I said. "No, I'll stay where I am."

ACTOR 1/MAC BRYAN: A black woman was riding with Lawrence and his crowd, and she's sitting in the black section like she's supposed to be and everything, and she's watching this dialogue between the bus-driver and Lawrence. And she's saying—

ACTOR 10/BUS-RIDER (*spoken very fast, and just loud enough to be heard in the front of the bus, with increasing speed and urgency as she goes along*): Keep on white boy, keep on, keep on, you're doin' what's right boy, you keep right where you are, don't let up, don't let that white driver intimidate *you*, you just stick right where you are, 'cause you're in your rights, you're a white boy, you stay right where you are!

ACTOR 1/MAC BRYAN (*Smiling*): And she's really lettin' the *whoooole* busload know what the truth is, right? And the bus driver's saying,

ACTOR 2/BUS-DRIVER: Lady where do you get off? Where do you get—how soon you get off this bus? Cause I'm gonna *put* you off if you don't shut up!

ACTOR 1/MAC BRYAN: She finally gets to her getting-off place, and she goes down the steps as slooowly as she can *parade* her dignity, and she gets to the bottom of the step—the bus-driver's saying—

ACTOR 2/BUS-DRIVER (*shooing her off*): Get off, get off, I've got a schedule I've got to meet!

ACTOR 1/MAC BRYAN: The black woman looks at the bus-driver in the face, she says—

ACTOR 10/BUS-RIDER: Mr. Bus-driver, don't you worry. *God* has a schedule too.

ACTOR 1/MAC BRYAN *(big smile, elated)*: Doesn't that sound like something straight out of Amos? "Ah don't worry, buddy, God has a schedule *too!*"

COUNTERPOINT: WATCHING MY MOTHER CRY

ACTOR 7/ THELMA DILLARD: *(Macon Councilperson. Strong, animated, confident)*: My mom, grandmother and I got on a bus, and the bus driver said to my grandmother: *(gruff voice)* "Hurry and sit down woman! Move to the back of the bus."
My mom went to the back of the bus. And tears rolled down her cheek, because her mother was treated so harshly—this humble, loving lady.

(Pause.)

And I sat there and watched my mother cry. And my grandmother said, "That's alright honey. I'm used to it."

WHO IS MY MOTHER?

ACTOR 3/STUDENT: *Combustible/Burn*, third principle:

ACTOR 4/STUDENT: "We stand for the free—

ACTOR 2/STUDENT: honest—

ACTOR 5/STUDENT: and rigorous pursuit of Truth

ACTOR 3/STUDENT: and the exchange of ideas in a fearless forum."

ACTOR 4/STUDENT: The truth?

ACTOR 2/STUDENT: My grandfather was an arch-segregationist. He was absolutely astounded at my views and was ready to disown me.

ACTOR 4/STUDENT: My mother heard about my activism on race at Mercer, wrote me a *letter*. She called me an ugly duckling.

ACTOR 3/STUDENT: My parents were upset and thought that I might be getting into a cult.

ACTOR 5/STUDENT: My mother had my church pray for me.

ACTOR 6/STUDENT: My Dad was a Deacon in the First Baptist Church of Gainesville, and he would just get so upset when I'd get on the race issue, that he would run to the bathroom and throw up. And mother would say—

ACTOR 4/MOTHER: See what you've done? His ulcer's going to bleed again, and you'll be the cause of it!

ACTOR 1/MAC BRYAN *(Smiling)*: See, Jesus was terribly hard on the family.

(ACTORS 2 and 5 approach ACTOR 3/JESUS.)

They came to Him and said:

ACTOR 2: Your mother and your brothers want you to get out of this business of talking on the street corner.

ACTOR 5: You're saying all those radical things!

ACTOR 1/MAC BRYAN: What does Jesus say? *(lamely)* "Oh sorry, I'm going to go home and cry?" No, no, He says—

ACTOR 3/JESUS *(challenging)*: Who is my mother and my brother?

ACTOR 1/MAC BRYAN *(laughs hard)*: That's a good question. "Who *is* my mother and my brother"? Nuclear family was *gone.* In that statement, the nuclear family was gone.

ACTOR 4/NANCY ATTAWAY HOLLOWAY (*Mercer class of 1956)*: My father and I didn't get along too well. I think I had an anti-authoritarian streak in me that was much stronger than it was in my other sisters: I was always the one kind of rockin' the boat, stirring up things.

Well when we would go through the black bottom in my town, the black ghetto—dirt roads, one shotgun little house after another—I would feel so guilty about that. The racism. It was just a community in the South living in total denial—it was like there was a dead dog in the middle of the dining room table and nobody wanted to acknowledge it.

Early on, I knew there was something the matter. But after I went to Mercer, Mac just touched a nerve within me. Then I really got radical, and was going to work with American Friends up in Atlanta, and my father, I mean, his true colors *(little laugh)* literally came out. He found out it was going to be an *interracial* group, and he got our congressman to investigate them, and told me I wasn't goin to do that. He said:

ACTOR 2/FATHER: You goin to—you goin to work in that group this summer, you'll end up bringing home a nigger to marry and I'll have to shoot him!

ACTOR 4/NANCY ATTAWAY HOLLOWAY *(looking at her father)*: I didn't say anything back.

(Pause. To the audience.)

I moved to Atlanta that summer and worked with the project. *(Mischievous smile.)*

COUNTERPOINT: AN ANGER DEFERRED

(ACTORS 7, 8, & 10 stand together, hovering over ACTOR 9, who plays MARK GLOVER. GLOVER is an elderly farmer, sitting on Third Street in Macon, selling butter beans. He speaks in a gravelly middle-Georgia accent. The women's voices are cobbled from interviews with CATHERINE MEEKS, ERNESTINE COLE, MAUREEN WALKER, BETTY J. WALKER, among others.)

ACTOR 9/MARK GLOVER: Back down then, they thought, well, this is the way they had to live—

ACTOR 7/AFRICAN AMERICAN WOMAN: My grandmother mainly taught tolerance—

ACTOR 9/MARK GLOVER: They wouldn't sell you a Co-cola—

ACTOR 8/AFRICAN AMERICAN WOMAN: It was the way things were—

ACTOR 9/MARK GLOVER: They'd sell you a Pepsi-cola. They wouldn't sell you a Coca-Cola—

ACTOR 10/AFRICAN AMERICAN WOMAN: My grandmother taught me to be patient—

ACTOR 9/MARK GLOVER: They'd say "Co-cola that's a white man's drink"—

ACTOR 10/AFRICAN AMERICAN WOMAN: Not necessarily to accept things, but to tolerate things as they were—

ACTOR 7/AFRICAN AMERICAN WOMAN: They had no choice. They had to try to keep from being killed—

ACTOR 9/MARK GLOVER: We used to talk about the Ku Klux. That what they were scared of. They used to come to the yard and call you out and kill you—

ACTOR 8/AFRICAN AMERICAN WOMAN: My family was struggling to make enough money to buy food—

ACTOR 9/MARK GLOVER: They wouldn't vote, they wouldn't vote! But I used to tell to tell them, I said "I don't care if you're not gonna vote. I'm ready, I'm going to vote." *(mimicking an outraged elderly person)* "Wahhl, well you get killed!"

ACTOR 7/AFRICAN AMERICAN WOMAN: They just knew they had a place and they stayed in it. My parents developed this real survival strategy:

ACTOR 10/AFRICAN AMERICAN WOMAN: Just don't let it get you all—

ACTORS 7-10: upset.

ACTOR 8/AFRICAN AMERICAN WOMAN: You know, you've got to—

ACTORS 7-10: Be patient—

ACTOR 7/AFRICAN AMERICAN WOMAN: You've got to—

ACTORS 7-10: Be careful—

ACTOR 9/AFRICAN AMERICAN WOMAN: (*politely*) Yessah—

ACTOR 7/AFRICAN AMERICAN WOMAN: —of what you say.

ACTOR 9/MARK GLOVER: My daddy told me about how the Ku Klux would tell them about, "don't you vote!"

ACTORS 7-10: Don't let it get you upset—

ACTOR 8/AFRICAN AMERICAN WOMAN (*politely*): No suh—

ACTOR 9/ MARK GLOVER: And they they they get 'em at night, come in the yard and get 'em at night and kill 'em—

ACTORS 7-10: Don't let it get you upset—

ACTOR 9/ MARK GLOVER: But I wanted that right—

ACTORS 7-10: Don't let it get you—

ACTOR 10/AFRICAN AMERICAN WOMAN: I didn't get angry—

ACTORS 7-10: Don't let it get you—

ACTOR 9/ MARK GLOVER: I wanted my rights—

ACTORS 2/WHITE MAN (*from the opposite side of the stage*): God's wish was separation of the races!

ACTORS 7-10: Don't let it get you upset!

ACTORS 3/WHITE MAN: Thy daughter—

ACTORS 1-6: *Thou shalt not*!

ACTOR 3/WHITE MAN: Give unto his son—

ACTORS 7-10: Don't let it get you—

ACTOR 9/ MARK GLOVER: I wanted that right, and I *ready*!

ACTORS 7-10: Don't let it get you upset!

ACTOR 10/AFRICAN AMERICAN WOMAN: So I didn't get angry... I didn't get angry until later on.

Koinonia

ACTOR 3/STUDENT: *Combustible/Burn,* fourth principle:

ACTOR 6/STUDENT: "We stand for a minimum standard of living—

ACTOR 2/STUDENT: based on the necessities, rather than the luxuries of life—

ACTOR 5/STUDENT: complete sharing—

ACTOR 4/STUDENT: beginning in our homes—

ACTOR 3/STUDENT: of the things we own with our brethren who sacrifice—

ACTOR 6/STUDENT: and our neighbors who need."

ACTOR 5/STUDENT: Complete sharing.

ACTOR 1/MAC: Mercer had a ruling made by some of the religion department people that Clarence Jordan, the co-founder of Koinonia Farms, could not speak on the campus. Now, that's official instruction. So what do we do? (*Smiles*) We go to Koinonia, an hour and a half southwest in Americus, Georgia.

(*African American workers and white workers side by side working on the farm. ACTOR 2 shovels vigorously, ACTOR 7 picks blueberries, ACTOR 6 gathers pecans, ACTOR 10 tills the soil, ACTOR 4 plants seeds, ACTOR 3 milks a cow. ACTOR 1 puts on a straw hat and becomes CLARENCE JORDAN. He should also work. The actors speak their lines as they work. The stage space, for the first time, should be fully integrated.*)

ACTOR 2/STUDENT: Clarence had a degree in Agriculture from the University of Georgia. He went to Southern Baptist Seminary—

ACTOR 7/ KOINONIAN: and became a Greek scholar—

ACTOR 10/KOINONIAN: fell in love with the Greek New Testament—

ACTOR 6/STUDENT: and so he came back and wanted to start something like the early church—

ACTOR 7/ KOINONIAN: in rural Southwest Georgia—

ACTOR 4/STUDENT: Can you believe that he came to Sumter County Georgia, 1942, and started a *commune* that was both integrated and pacifist in the middle of the world war?

EVERYONE ON STAGE: Koinonia.

ACTOR 10/KOINONIAN: It means fellowship in the Greek—-

ACTOR 3/STUDENT: Black and white people out in the farm working together, getting hot in the Georgia sun—

ACTOR 6/STUDENT: Inter-racial—

ACTOR 7/KOINONIAN: Inter-denominational—

ACTOR 4/STUDENT: Clarence was the person closest to Jesus of anybody I've ever known.

ACTOR 2/STUDENT: He was a Baptist! (*laughs*) There were a few Baptists in the world. *Christian* Baptists—

ACTOR 6/STUDENT: And they believed in the New Testament church where you give up everything and you're a community.

ACTOR 1/CLARENCE JORDAN: We committed ourselves to equality of fellowship, economically and otherwise, and that meant, of course, having a common purse.

ACTOR 7/KOINONIAN: They thought he was communist—

ACTOR 1/CLARENCE JORDAN: We pooled all that we had and made distribution on the basis of need and not on the basis of greed or knowledge or power or anything.

ACTOR 4/STUDENT: What was surprising was that each family who had their own little house out there had abundance.

ACTOR 2/STUDENT: There was no poverty there.

ACTOR 6/STUDENT: To me that was ideal as over against the organized church, which was just like another social part of your life that helped your status in the community.

ACTOR 2/STUDENT: Clarence was saying that God expects us to follow Christ—

ACTOR 4/STUDENT: not sit in the fancy pews in comfort and worship Christ, but to follow Him—

ACTOR 3/STUDENT: not one day, one hour a week. It was your total life.

ACTOR 6/STUDENT: That blew my mind.

ACTOR 1/MAC BRYAN: And we have the time of our lives at Koinonia. Living in poverty. Drinking out of tin cans. Sitting on nail kegs. Having the highest theological world discussion—far beyond what the university was doing.

EVERYONE ON STAGE: Koinonia.

(Everyone stops working and gathers at a central table for dinner.)

ACTOR 2/STUDENT: Then we walked over to the common mess and sat on little benches to eat, three or four people on each side—

ACTOR 4/STUDENT: Black and white together—

(The actors sit down at the table, and everyone bows their heads. ACTOR 7 begins to say a prayer of thanks.)

ACTOR 7/KOINONIAN: Most wonderful and merciful heavenly God. We pray this evening God that you will give us love, that we should give each other care and each other love. And God accept thanks for this food we have received. Amen.

EVERYONE ON STAGE: Amen.

ACTOR 10/KOINONIAN: Yeah, this was paradise—

ACTOR 8/KOINONIAN: Here everybody was the same: we laugh, we talk, we eat, we play together—

ACTOR 9/ALMA JACKSON *(An Americus farmer and former Koinonian)*: When the Mercer students came down, we'd have a square dance down there together, black and white—

ACTOR 6/STUDENT: Word spread around Sumter County of white men taking their meals with a Negro, dancing with Negroes.

(The actors suddenly separate, recreating the color line. They take all chairs save one from the table, transforming the table into an interrogation stand. ACTOR 2 regards ACTOR 9 from an elevated platform.)

ACTOR 9/ALMA JACKSON: I had to go before a grand jury. They were having a big investigation on Koinonia, and they were asking questions. And one old man, boy, you could just see hate in him, boy he was turnin' red. He asked me:

ACTOR 2/OLD MAN: Who did you dance with?

ACTOR 9/ALMA JACKSON: I dance with my wife.

ACTOR 2/OLD MAN: Where are the white people when you're dancing?

ACTOR 9/ALMA JACKSON: They'd be there sometimes.

ACTOR 2/OLD MAN: Don't you all exchange partners?

ACTOR 9/ALMA JACKSON: Yeah, we exchange partners.

ACTOR 2/OLD MAN *(insinuating)*: Well, you ever dance with one of them white women?

ACTOR 9/ALMA JACKSON: Yeah, just a little bit.

ACTOR 2/OLD MAN: Well, don't you like that, holding a white woman's hand?

ACTOR 9/ALMA JACKSON: I said, "I don't know if I do or not."

ACTOR 2/OLD MAN: Where you get money for the dance?

ACTOR 9/ALMA JACKSON *(addressing the audience)*: You didn't call nobody mister or misses down here at Koinonia. You call by their name, you know, and nothing was thought about it. So I said, "I get it from Florence Jordan."

ACTOR 2/OLD MAN: *Who?*

ACTOR 9/ALMA JACKSON: Florence Jordan—

ACTOR 2/OLD MAN *(loud)*: *Who did you say?*

ACTOR 9/ALMA JACKSON: Florence Jordan.

ACTOR 2/OLD MAN: Who's wife is that? Isn't that Clarence's wife?

ACTOR 9/ALMA JACKSON: Yes it is.

ACTOR 2/OLD MAN: You mean you call that white woman by her first name?

ACTOR 9/ALMA JACKSON: I said, "Yes, that what she told me to call her."

ACTOR 2/OLD MAN *(Enraged)*: Boy, what do you think were to happen to you if you were callin a white woman by her name that wasn't down there at that farm?

ACTOR 9/ALMA JACKSON: I said, *(soft)* "I don't know."

ACTOR 6/STUDENT: And you know that the Klan would have to respond—

ACTOR 9/ALMA JACKSON: They burned a cross at my mother's house and then they set the house on fire. About ten or eleven o'clock at night. They spread gas across the porch. Put a cotton pillow out there with a gallon jug of gasoline in it. Set it on fire. And it was supposed to burn slow and then explode. My mother and my brother-in-law put it out before it exploded. And then the sheriff told her:

ACTOR 2/SHERIFF: The reason that's happening to *you*, because that boy you've got is living over there at that farm. If he was to leave, they'd leave you alone.

ACTOR 10/KOINONIAN: Most of the black people were afraid to work here, because if they found out they were working here and living on this place—

ACTOR 7/KOINONIAN: You were in danger.

ACTOR 8/KOINONIAN: Your life was in danger.

ACTOR 9/ALMA JACKSON: And it was just—things just started falling apart you know. And I just left—

ACTOR 7/KOINONIAN: And then there was a big boycott of Koinonia produce—

COMBUSTIBLE/BURN

ACTOR 8/KOINONIAN: And then they burnt up and dynamited the roadside market—

ACTOR 7/KOINONIAN: Plus they had Clarence's insurance canceled—

ACTOR 9/KOINONIAN: And he couldn't borrow money from the bank. They did everything they could to get him away from here—

ACTOR 2/STUDENT: They started firing shot-guns—firing shots into the farm—

ACTOR 1/CLARENCE JORDAN: One day, the Klan paid a call at Koinonia. A couple of gentlemen came, said they had been sent by the Ku Klux Klan. And they said:

ACTOR 3/KLANSMAN: We want to come right to the point with you. We want to let you know that we don't let the sun set on any white man that eats with a nigger!

ACTOR 1/CLARENCE JORDAN: And I put on my broadest smile and stuck out my hand and said, "well, I'm a Baptist preacher, I'm just so happy to meet you. All my life I've wanted to meet some people who had power over the sun. We will be watching it with great interest tonight."

(Gun fire rings out.)

ACTOR 8/KOINONIAN: Before night was over they raked that farm with machine gun fire.

ACTOR 7/STUDENT: "On January 9, 1957, machine-gun bullets tore through the house, and two days later the night-riders returned, spraying bullets this time at a volleyball court where a cluster of Koinonia children were playing."

(A photo of children, African American and white, standing together on Koinonia farms.)

ACTOR 10/KOINONIAN: Koinonia never retaliated.

A FRIENDLY, DANGEROUS PLACE

ACTOR 2/MILLARD FULLER *(founder of Habitat for Humanity and former Koinonian)*: There was a man from India who came to Koinonia—he was Hindu. So he got curious and said: "I would like to go to church." So the Koinonians went to a little Baptist church near Koinonia. And the church people were *not* happy. They had a meeting and voted the Jordans out of the church for bringing in this "black" man. They said he broke up the fine spirit of Christian unity.

(Pause.)

All of my life I always thought of the church as a happy, positive, safe place. Then I came to Koinonia, and I saw if you don't conform exactly to the cultural expectations, you can get in big trouble. I saw the church could be a *dangerous* place.

THE LITTLE CHILDREN OF THE WORLD

ACTOR 1/MAC BRYAN: Baptists in Georgia, see, they *never* took a stand. And what was happening, see—these were all Baptist students for the most part—and they were saying "*why—is—our—denomination*—the largest, most prominent denomination—not saying a word!" See. That's the conspiracy of silence.

ACTOR 5/STUDENT: *Combustible/Burn,* fifth principle:

ACTOR 2/STUDENT: "We stand for the ecumenical fellowship of Christians—

ACTOR 6/STUDENT: Fellowship—

ACTOR 4/STUDENT: as over against narrow creeds—

ACTOR 3/STUDENT: and institutional denominations."

ACTORS 3, 4, 5 and 6/STUDENTS: Institutional Christians.

ACTOR 6/STUDENT: We went to church every Sunday—

ACTOR 4/STUDENT: My daddy was a deacon of the church—

ACTOR 2/STUDENT: My mother taught Sunday school and spoke in churches—

ACTOR 6/STUDENT: I never once heard from any minister a question about how we were treating black people—

ACTOR 3/STUDENT: Not one time—

ACTOR 5/STUDENT: Nothing—

ACTOR 4/STUDENT: It never came up.

ACTOR 3/STUDENT: The gospel had been kidnapped—

ACTOR 2/STUDENT: The only thing that really made an impression was that this world was no good—

ACTOR 4/STUDENT: And the next world was the reward for this world.

ACTOR 6/STUDENT: They had no understanding at all of the good that can happen in *this* world—

ACTOR 3/STUDENT: Our world.

ACTOR 5/STUDENT: Mother took me to church all the time. Baptist church—

ACTOR 2/STUDENT: I grew up in Atlanta in the Highland area. I grew up there and we'd walk to Druid Hills Baptist Church—

ACTOR 5/STUDENT: And I remember thinking probably when I was eight or nine that. . . there was something just nnnnnot right, because we'd go to—to Sunday school and sing—

ACTOR 2/STUDENT: —that song: "Jesus loves the little children of the world,

ACTORS 5 & 2: Red and yellow, black and white—

ACTOR 5/STUDENT: They are precious in His sight."

(ACTORS 8 & 9 sing softly in the background, "red and yellow, black and white, they are precious in His sight.")

ACTOR 2/STUDENT: We'd sing it every week almost. And then we had colored and white bathrooms in the church—

ACTOR 5/STUDENT: I was aware of the signs in the city, you know—

ACTOR 2/STUDENT: The church required me to bus the kids miles and miles away to an all white swimming pool. We could have gone over very close, within walking distance of the church, but it had integrated.

ACTOR 5/STUDENT: For some reason I was conscious that something was not, not right in my town.

ACTOR 2/STUDENT: That really upset me.

(The actors stop singing.)

COUNTERPOINT: IF JESUS CAME BACK

ACTOR 10/REV. LONZY EDWARDS *(Pastor at Mount Mariah Baptist Church, Macon and Attorney at Law. He speaks in the quietly intense voice of a preacher and a scholar)*: A lot of folk in the white community emphasize an understanding of religion that almost has nothing to do with social justice. For a lot of white brethren, I think the suspicion that some of us have had is that the whole focus was "don't engage in pre-marital sex, don't smoke and don't drink," and that sort of thing. And I don't have a problem with that. It's just that it's not the whole story.

For most black folk, there's a social dimension to the gospel. Our religion has basically been a religion of protest. It's had to be that. Our white brethren had what we were always trying to get. The idea of deliverance—of the Israelites from Egypt. Our best preachers always pick up on that. Themes of liberation. Justice.

(Listens to a question.)

Jesus? Today, Jesus would get run out of town. And if he got crowds in the wrong place, and started talking about feeding them, then people would probably accuse him of being a nuisance. Might get put in jail for disturbing the peace. The business community would say, "I'm trying to make a living man. You gotta carry these dead beats, vagabonds and folk like that, you gotta carry those folks somewhere else." The folk who use his name would probably react to him, would react to Jesus, the same way they would react whenever they heard Martin King was coming into town. It would not be a very pleasant thing.

MARY AND MARTHA

ACTOR 2/STUDENT: *Combustible/Burn:* no articulated principle concerning women's rights.

ACTOR 3/STUDENT: I think it was just implied that that there was no difference. Mac and Clarence made no overt statements or talk about women.

ACTOR 2/STUDENT: Women in the group were just as we were.

ACTOR 3/STUDENT: There was certainly no thinking that women must stay in their place at all. You know, their place was any place they wanted to be. (*chuckles*)

(*CAROLYN MARTIN, Mercer class of 1956, has a throaty, low laugh and a warm voice. Some facts have been slightly altered in this monologue in the interests of privacy.*)

ACTOR 6/CAROLYN MARTIN: I loved Koinonia farms and felt very welcome there. I remember Clarence in this rustic house, sitting in a straight chair talking *deep* theology, and of God's great love and the kingdom of God, and the kids were crawling all over him, and he never raised his voice. He just loved them and let them come and go and he kept talking.

The Koinonia women did not join in this. They were busy working. See that's been the story of my life—and I wanted to sit and listen to (*laughs*) what Clarence had to say, and instead I felt obligated to help make I think it was sixty egg salad sandwiches. Peeling the eggs and mashing 'em up and (*laughs*)

I didn't want to do it—but I never thought to question that. My husband and the men were talking with Clarence and I was busy working.

The story of my life: the Mary Martha parable in the bible. I always wanted to be Mary and I always felt that I ended up being Martha.

When I began Mac's class in my junior year, I was already married. When we were dating, Mercer had lots of rules. . . for girls. We had a twelve inch rule in the parlor in the women's dorm. We could sit on the love seats with the guys, but we had to be twelve inches apart. And one woman actually had a ruler and would come and measure. And what had happened in the parlor one day, the guy that wanted to be with me all the time, he had insisted on ah. . . going beyond the twelve inch rule. . . by a long shot *(laughs)*. And I knew we were going to get caught, and I was trying to get away, and I got up off the sofa and started to run out, and he grabbed me and pinned me to the wall. And when he did, that woman came by and campused me: the entire weekend, I couldn't leave my room. She said nothing to him.

My boyfriend was very possessive, showed up everywhere. I couldn't date anybody else, and it got to the point that, by the end of the sophomore year, I was either going to leave school, go home, break up or we'd have to get married. I was a strong girl. . . except Southern Baptists teach so *tremendously* well that females are to defer to males—to defer to authority.

And I was very naive. The first person that we as Southern Baptist girls had sexual impulses for, we believed we should marry. Nobody had ever talked to me about sex. My mother had given me a book written by Kotex and that was my indoctrination to growing up *(laughs)*. He was a very immature fellow and I was a very immature girl.

(Short pause.)

We married the next September.

If I had been honest, I felt it was a mistake as I walked down the aisle. But I thought *(slowly, emphasizing each word)* this—is—the—honorable—thing to do. And this is what I must do. . . as a good Baptist girl. I was nineteen, and Jack started running my life when I was seventeen. He even had me so that I was giving him my allowance and he was telling me how to spend it. He was making all my decisions.

After we were married, I thought that I was responsible for keeping him happy and keeping him at home, and ah, there was just no way to do that and not have sex. And I knew if we did, I'd probably get pregnant, no matter what I was doing. And it was the pre-pill generation. It was a very difficult thing.

(Pause.)

I had my first baby eleven months after we married. And Mercer's rules were that I could not go to school if I was pregnant, even married. I had to wear a raincoat every day winter quarter to keep people from seeing that I was pregnant. I couldn't keep going to school anyway. I wanted to, but I was expected to work to put my husband through medical school. I had to sacrifice my dreams. And all along I was to be gracious. This—*this* is the real crux: is believing that this is something that you're *supposed* to be doing and be gracious—*(suddenly, breaking in as if in pain, physically shocked)* oh—*ohhh* you have sparked something. Let me tell you this.

(Pause.)

Oh. It hurts. I was seven and a half months pregnant with my first child, and at some point at one of Mac's weekly meetings, we had sentence prayers. And I began to cry. I was crying because I felt very badly of myself. How could I be such an ingrate? And such an immature girl, instead of a *"woman."* And I prayed that God would help make me. . . accepting. And not to be resentful that I could not continue my education. I had never had my mind so stretched. . . but I could not continue being the kind of person I had been in the group with Mac. A-ha. (*whispered*) Yeah. I had to give it all up. I was a wife and mother: I had to give up everything for my husband. My life now. . . would be living *through* my husband and my children. Not me. (*Pause.*) I no longer had a life of my own.

(*Long pause.*)

I had a tubaligation in '59 after my fourth baby died and, ah, it took ten doctor's signatures plus my husband's for me to get the surgery. They were all men.

(*Pause.*)

I didn't even have rights over my own body.

ACTOR 4/STUDENT: Mac, what is justice?

ACTOR 1/MAC BRYAN: I say to my wife "I love you love you love you!" and I grab her and hug her and throw her up in the air and before she hits the ground she says, "who gets the car keys?" See, you have one car. And that's justice, see. You know, it's very simple. Justice is very simple. All you have to do is ask who gets the car keys?

SILENT CONSPIRACIES

ACTOR 2/STUDENT: *Combustible/Burn*, sixth principle:

ACTOR 5/STUDENT: "We stand for alternatives to war—

ACTOR 3/STUDENT: iron-curtain propaganda—

ACTOR 5/STUDENT: war—

ACTOR 4/STUDENT: nationalistic patriotism—

ACTOR 6/STUDENT: and armaments—

ACTOR 5/STUDENT: war—

ACTOR 6/STUDENT: This may be the path of all-out pacifism—

ACTOR 4/STUDENT: or lesser degrees of variation upon that."

ACTOR 5/STUDENT: Peace.

ACTOR 3/EINAR MICHAELSON (*Mercer class of 1951. He speaks in a soft-spoken working class New York accent of an earlier era.*): I came out of a fundamentalist background. Very traditional. I think I had one session of high school. Because my family was poor, I went to New York when I was fifteen, got a job in order to feed the family.

(*We are in a busy factory, several actors soundlessly miming strenuous work activities.*)

During World War II, I was a tool maker with Grumann aircraft out in Long Island. We made carrier-based planes. And um, ehhh—and I don't know what hap—one day—I'm working at my bench, and em—

(*Exhales. The factory sounds stop, but everyone continues to work silently.*)

I… everything came quiet. Here I'm working in a shop: ma*chin*ery going, *people* are *ham*mering, and all kinds of things are going on. (*All factory workers freeze.*) Everything *stops*. . . for me.

(Pause.)

Aaand I am overcome with guilt. *(Pause. Slowly.)* Because I am making an instrument that will kill people and destroy God's creation.

(Pause.)

And I don't know what to do. I am overcome by it.

(Pause.)

And eh (*breathes out*) I sort of made a vow. I said, "well, *(slowly)* the first chance I get I want to do something to help people not destroy people." Why it happened, *(faster)* I have—I can't—I have no reason for it. None at all. It came. And it stayed with me after the war was over. Like an itch I couldn't scratch. It's nothing that I could put my finger on. I couldn't show it to anybody. I couldn't even explain it. It was just *there*. And I couldn't shake it *off*.

ACTOR 1/MAC BRYAN: Einar got a job teaching at a black college in Macon—

ACTOR 3/EINAR MICHAELSON: I taught at a Negro college—the Georgia Baptist Junior College in Macon, over on Gray Highway—

ACTOR 1/MAC BRYAN: It's now deceased—see, that college was set up deliberately to evade Mercer's desegregation. The buildings were so run down that our Koinonia group would go over on weekends and repair them.

ACTOR 6/STUDENT: There were very few buildings, dilapidated buildings. The only equipment that we saw for the science classroom was a—almost a toy microscope. And the books were all old. The yard was bare.

ACTOR 3/EINAR MICHAELSON: I was on the faculty there, and my salary came from the Southern Baptist Convention, which was white.

ACTOR 6/STUDENT: And my heart was just heavy, really—I—it *hurt* to go there and see what those kids had, and what we had.

ACTOR 3/EINAR MICHAELSON: Well, I preached at a white church on mother's day. I spoke about segregation by using scriptures—both the Hebrew and the Christian scriptures—showing them that segregation shouldn't exist. *(pause)* And they didn't like what I said. And they wrote to the headquarters of the Southern Baptist Convention—

ACTOR 1/MAC BRYAN: And the board of trustees made up of Baptist members in Macon—you know, bankers, and lawyers, all white—and they heard what Einar was doing, and they came down and said "you're fired." Just like that, said "you're fired."

ACTOR 3/EINAR MICHAELSON: —and discontinued my salary. Gee, I was shocked! Really. That they would do this.

ACTOR 1/MAC BRYAN: And one of the saddest sights I've ever seen. . . was the night Einar came to our house in a rented trailer, with his three kids and all of his household goods. And he was telling us goodbye. Crying. *(Beat.)* All of them. *(Beat.)* Sad. *(Beat.)* They expected to spend their lives in Georgia. He was exiled. Told there's no place for you around here.

REMNANTS

(JOE HENDRICKS, Mercer class of 1955, was Director of Religious Activities at Mercer from 1959-1962, Dean of Men from 1961-1970, and Assistant Professor of Christianity, 1959-2000. Unlike MAC, JOE comes across as entirely laid back, yet firm in his convictions. He wears jeans and a blue button-down shirt. His voice is a deep, slow gravel. His hands are constantly in motion—not frenetic, but slowly and specifically gestural, used to make major points.)

ACTOR 2/JOE HENDRICKS: The majority of students at Mercer in the fifties were not Bryanites. You must keep this in mind. Getting a term from the Hebrew bible, these students were a remnant. You're talking about five percent of the student body who were operating that way.

I'll give you an example. There was an occurrence at Tatnall Square Park right across from Willingham over there, about a stone's throw from this theater. As I remember rightly what had happened was some little black kids had wandered into T-square park. Pre-school. Little tots. So a white man was enraged about it—blacks were banned from the park—and I don't know who called them, but here comes the police. And so Bill Randall and Louis Wynne—both African Americans—had come into the park to try to get the kids out of the park, to protect them. And Louis went out there and this white man stabbed him.

(ACTOR 3 stabs ACTOR 9.)

Right there in the park. Now all along the front of Mercer—now, this is something you need to remember about this—all the way from Tatnall Square church all the way to the corner—was filled with Mercer students cheering the white man that had stabbed Louis.

Louis had a whole bunch of stitches put in. But he was a World War II veteran. He wasn't a stranger to combat.

ACTOR 7/NARRATOR: From letters to the editor published in the Mercer *Cluster* during the 1950's and 60's:

ACTOR 3/SEGREGATIONIST STUDENT: I have nothing whatsoever against a Negro. It is the "White Negro" that makes my stomach crawl. Who are these white Negroes? They are white people who are dying to serve, love, and mix with Negroes. They are people who want to integrate.

ACTOR 2/SEGREGATIONIST STUDENT: Without beating around the bush, the present editor of the *Cluster* stands counter the admittance of Negroes. . . Can't the government supply the Negro race colleges of their own rather than admitting them to ours?

ACTOR 4/SEGREGATIONIST STUDENT: One of the most popular reasons for segregation on this campus is that Negro enrollment would cause intermarriage.

ACTOR 3/SEGREGATIONIST STUDENT: My blood is entirely white, for I have NO desire to mix with ANY OTHER blood whatsoever.

ACTOR 1/SEGREGATIONIST STUDENT: What white woman would in all pride have a Negro baby?

ACTOR 3/SEGREGATIONIST STUDENT: I predict that in the immediate future we will be ruled by "darkies"—

ACTOR 5/SEGREGATIONIST STUDENT: That is when I will laugh at all you Negro lovers—

ACTOR 4/SEGREGATIONIST STUDENT: If there be those who think they can do more for the Negro by freely mixing with him, and so desire, then I suggest that they cross the color line in the color direction.

ACTOR 1/SEGREGATIONIST STUDENT: As a means of identification, I suggest they wear black stars so that we might be made aware of their departure from us until such time as they have become completely amalgamated.

ACTOR 5/SEGREGATIONIST STUDENT: Who discovered this country?

ACTOR 3/SEGREGATIONIST STUDENT: Who settled this country?

ACTOR 4/SEGREGATIONIST STUDENT: Who made this country what it is today?

ACTOR 1/SEGREGATIONIST STUDENT: You're exactly right:

ACTOR 2/SEGREGATIONIST STUDENT: The White Race!

ACTOR 1/SEGREGATIONIST STUDENT: Who is slowly but surely losing control of our great nation?

ACTOR 5/SEGREGATIONIST STUDENT: The White—

ACTOR 3/SEGREGATIONIST STUDENT: The White—

ACTOR 2/SEGREGATIONIST STUDENT: The White—

ACTORS 2, 3, 4, & 5: The White Race!

ANDREW SILVER

ACTOR 1/SEGREGATIONIST STUDENT (*to the audience*): What part will you play? The down-fall, or the advancement of our nation?

Cookout

ACTOR 6/STUDENT: *Combustible/Burn*, seventh principle:

ACTOR 4/STUDENT: We will accept each person for what he—or she—is.

ACTOR 2/CLIFFORD YORK: On May 17, 1954 the Brown versus the Board of Education Supreme Court decision took place. That was the year that I graduated from college. And that summer—

ACTOR 3/FURMAN YORK (*Mercer Class of 1958. Furman speaks in his brother's Georgia mountain accent, only more playful, more excited, and much faster*): My brother Cliff and I rented a little place on the West Ridge Circle. A navy man and his family were gone for the summer, so we were all staying there. And I got a job at Sears downtown and I met, uh. . . I will use the term I used back then. I would call him an African American today, but he was a "Negro" back then. His name was Richard Scott.

ACTOR 9/RICHARD SCOTT (*Talladega graduate, later road-manager for the Supremes, manager of New Kids on the Block, actor and producer. He has a relaxed, imperturbable voice*): I was a junior at Talledega College. One summer I came home from college and I took a job at Sears Roebuck. And I was a carpet cutter, measuring and cutting carpets, and one of the white fellas also worked with me there. We were friends—

ACTOR 3/FURMAN YORK: I liked him and he liked me—

ACTOR 9/RICHARD SCOTT: And once he invited to me to his house—

ACTOR 3/FURMAN YORK: Richard came out to my house—

ACTOR 9/RICHARD SCOTT: The boy and I had become really good friends—

ACTOR 3/FURMAN YORK: And we were playing croquet—

ACTOR 9/RICHARD SCOTT: You know, it was *fun*—

ACTOR 3/FURMAN YORK: Started the hamburgers going at West Ridge Circle—

ACTOR 9/RICHARD SCOTT: It felt like a natural thing to do, you know?

ACTOR 3/FURMAN YORK: My brother came home—

ACTOR 2/CLIFFORD YORK: At the end of a *very* hot Macon day in the summer. And we talked—

ACTOR 3/FURMAN YORK: And then the phone rang—

ACTOR 2/CLIFFORD YORK: And then the phone rang—

ACTOR 9/RICHARD SCOTT: And then the phone rang—

ACTOR 3/FURMAN YORK: And it said something like this:

ACTOR 1/NEIGHBOR: Get that nigger out of there. *(pause.)*

ACTOR 3/FURMAN YORK: And it was shocking. And now remember: I am a little snotty nosed boy from Clayton,

Georgia, and I haven't been to Mercer for four years like my brother, and I haven't studied with Mac Bryan.

ACTOR 2/CLIFFORD YORK: And Furman came out and said—

ACTOR 3/FURMAN YORK: This is something you better handle.

ACTOR 2/CLIFFORD YORK: Hello?

ACTOR 1/NEIGHBOR *(in the darkness)*: Get that nigger out of our neighborhood right away— out of our backyards.

ACTOR 9/RICHARD SCOTT: Somebody told me later that some neighbor had seen some of us on the back porch—and saw me standing there.

ACTOR 2/CLIFFORD YORK: And I'd seen blacks in the community. Every day they hung the laundry, they mowed the lawn, they did all kinds of labor works and menial tasks for the white folks there. And I said, kind of an idealist, I said: "First of all, he is not a nigger. He is a Ne-gro. And he is my guest." And he said—

ACTOR 1/NEIGHBOR: Well, you better get him out or I'm going to call the police.

ACTOR 2/CLIFFORD YORK: And I said, "Well, you do whatever you have to do."

ACTOR 3/FURMAN YORK: In a little while the police came.

(ACTOR 1 slowly makes his way to the door.)

The police came to our door—knocked on our door—and said—

ACTOR 1/POLICEMAN: We have to arrest you guys. You've—You've broken an unwritten law.

ACTOR 2/CLIFFORD YORK: Well, I said "what is that?"

ACTOR 1/POLICEMAN: You have this uh—We hear you have a nigger in your house as your guest, and there's an unwritten law against that.

ACTOR 3/FURMAN YORK: And my brother—a little more sophisticated than me, right, he said—

ACTOR 2/CLIFFORD YORK: Well, do you have a warrant for our arrest? And he says no, and he started to reach for the screen door—I remember this vividly—and when he did, I made out like I was latching it, and he didn't know that the latch was broken. So all I did was hold it with my finger, and he stopped. And I said: "Why don't you get a warrant for our arrest?" And he said—

ACTOR 1/POLICEMAN: Well that's no problem.

ACTOR 2/CLIFFORD YORK: And his partner went back out to the police car and called, and I said, "It's hot, why don't you guys come in, and I'll give you some iced-tea?"

ACTOR 3/FURMAN YORK: So my brother invited the first policeman in while the other one went to get a warrant.

(The POLICEMAN, CLIFFORD and FURMAN all sit down together in the living room. Tense.)

ACTOR 2/CLIFFORD YORK: I was trying to be Christianly toward them as Mac Bryan had taught us—

ACTOR 3/FURMAN YORK: And Richard, who was a musical person, played the piano for him.

(RICHARD SCOTT *sits at the piano. Moonlight Sonata begins to play*)

ACTOR 2/CLIFFORD YORK: I asked Richard if he'd play some music on the piano while we were waiting. It was Beethoven—

ACTOR 9/RICHARD SCOTT (*playing*): The Moonlight Sonata.

ACTOR 2/CLIFFORD YORK: So he played classical music on that piano, and I thought, "God, I could never play that if I lived to be a hundred."

(*Pause.*)

And it was beautiful music.

(*Pause. The sonata continues.*)

I think deep down inside, the policeman must have seen that this was an awkward situation. I mean, he probably didn't understand it any more than I did but, you know, I think you kind of know in your heart that that's beautiful music. And nobody said a word. Nothing.

(*The sonata continues.*)

It wasn't long until they came with a warrant for our arrest. They went out and talked awhile, and the policeman walked me over in the corner and he whispered to me, and he said:

ACTOR 1/POLICEMAN: Look, just give me the nigger, and, and, we'll just let—we'll just drop everything against you. We won't bother you.

ACTOR 2/CLIFFORD YORK: I could see them beating the hell out of that poor young man, you know, someplace between there and the police station, teaching him a lesson. And I just—I could not be a party to that. So I said, "I'm sorry, I can't do that."

ACTOR 3/FURMAN YORK: And they take my brother and they take Richard to jail.

ACTOR 9/RICHARD SCOTT: And they arrested me. And I remember them putting me in the car. They arrested the boy as well. And they took me down in a separate police car—we didn't even ride in the same car.

ACTOR 2/CLIFFORD YORK: And they took us down to the—the jail there in the square, and they searched us and took my chapstick—

ACTOR 3/FURMAN YORK: They even searched his chapstick. They took it apart like he was some kind of serious criminal.

ACTOR 9/RICHARD SCOTT: And I guess I was frightened, but I knew that I hadn't *done* anything, you know? What was more frightening is when they put me in the cell and locked me up.

ACTOR 2/CLIFFORD YORK: They took Richard in one direction, and they took me up the stairs to the top. And I found out later they called it the "Famed Skylight"—for violent prisoners. It was really a steel cell—they controlled the light on the outside. They opened the door and threw me in. I said, "Where's the light?" And he just laughed, said, "You don't get any light." Closed the door and it was total darkness.

(Black out. Then slowly, in the dark.)

It was. . . I wasn't afraid. Being a mountain boy, I—I don't get afraid easily. But it was hot. And total darkness. I could not see one crack out to look at the street light or anything else outside. It was so strange. Like a nightmare. The twilight zone.

ACTOR 5: From the *Macon Telegraph*, June 23, 1954:

ACTOR 7: "Clifford York, a white ministerial student, charged last night that he and a Negro pre-med student were taken into custody by Bibb sheriff's deputies who told them they had 'violated the segregation laws'. . . he was released after a friend called an attorney."

ACTOR 5: From the *Macon Telegraph*, June 29:

ACTOR 10: "Bibb Sheriff James Wood yesterday said he believed his deputies acted lawfully in the arrest last week of a white ministerial student and a Negro college graduate at a West Ridge circle residence."

ACTOR 1/SHERIFF JAMES WOOD: "An act legal within itself may become illegal if coupled with factors tending to produce a breach of the peace, to incite a riot or affray or to create a public nuisance. Good race relations have existed in this community for the last 10 or 15 years and the sheriff's office will continue to use any legal means to prevent racial disturbances here."

ACTOR 3/FURMAN YORK: Why don't you come out to our house for a cook out?

ACTOR 9/RICHARD SCOTT: I think my father said something about, "boy, don't you know you can't—you can't make it with those white boys." And I guess I never did anymore.

ACTOR 3/FURMAN YORK: I never heard from Richard again.

(*Moonlight Sonata, presto agitato plays, small white searchlights comb the stage, catching FURMAN and CLIFFORD, and then turning outwards to the audience.*)

ACTOR 1 (*unseen*): Nigger-lover!

ACTOR 5: Race-mixer!

ACTOR 1: We're going to get you, nigger-lover!

ACTOR 3/FURMAN YORK: So now what happened, what really settled in is, uh, really, fear. Every night, we had cars in the West Ridge Circle, hanging around, throwing spotlights on us.

ACTOR 2/CLIFFORD YORK: And they would spot our house at night and blow their horns.

ACTOR 3/FURMAN YORK: I slept with a knife. A butcher knife and a croquet mallet.

ACTOR 2/CLIFFORD YORK: And they would call and call and threaten us, and they would throw bricks, and rocks, and boxes, and trash and all that stuff in our front yard, and yell "nigger lover!" and all that kind of stuff. (*exhales*) It —it was—it was—that was tough. Because it was twenty-four hours a day kind of harassment from these people.

ACTOR 3/FURMAN YORK: And so for a long period of time we were threatened in every way.

ACTOR 2/CLIFFORD YORK: We went down to Jekyl Island for the weekend, and when we got back, Jan's roommate was out there and said—waiting for us—

ACTOR 4/ROOMMATE: Cliff you don't live there at West Ridge Circle any longer—the owner came down and threw everything you have out of the house and into the street.

ACTOR 2/CLIFFORD YORK: I got evicted. It happened that quickly.

(CLIFFORD sits down slowly.)

Troublemaker

ACTOR 3/FURMAN YORK: So they kicked us out. And when I went back to Clayton, Georgia, and when I went to visit home, guess what everybody called me? "The nigger lover is here." And I got all that from all my buddies that I grew up with. And my parents said, "You embarrassed us so much," you know, "we—we can't walk down the street without people looking funny at us." And interestingly enough, I pulled into a service station and one of the black persons who worked there, he came up to me and shook my hand.

(Pause.)

Do you want to know how—can I tell you two things here? The two things that influenced my life dramatically in terms of my future growth, and what have you? This was one of them. But the other was this: in my sophomore year at Mercer, I was coming from somewhere across campus. It was like 3:30 in the afternoon, and there was an ambulance. And they were carrying a body out on a stretcher. And uh, underneath it—the body was covered—but I could see very vividly—to this moment—it was a young man that had hanged himself by one of the pipes.

He was a gay person.

And that is a second incident that has really, really impacted me—that this guy was *so* unhappy, and had so much difficulty in adjusting, and so much stress and pressure. . . And so I have been very involved in, in the gay issue.

I've always been the troublemaker, if anything comes up that has to do with rights.

(Pause.)

The fifties were a really mellow period. I didn't see it as turbulent. But the seed was planted with a lot of people.

Sweet Potato Farm

ACTOR 2/JACK MCCLENDON *(Mercer class of 1952. He speaks in a distinctively urbane accent from an earlier era—an Alabaman Cary Grant)*: Mac turned my life upside down and inside out. See I was in the second world war and didn't know there were unpaved streets to black town. I didn't see those streets. I didn't see black people. I didn't see them until Mac showed me what they looked like. But his eyes had been opened too. And he doesn't tell you that much about that. He grew up in North Carolina, and one can hazard the guess that he was like I was at one point when he was growing up.

ACTOR 1/MAC BRYAN: I was a farm boy in the Depression. And we were living, you know, from hand to mouth. My father had just been in the eighth grade. And all his life never talked to me one time about what we're talking about now. We only talked about nature and farming and things like that.

So we're working in the field, and we're working in potatoes, we sell sweet potatoes, and we had to pick them up after they're plowed up. And they lie in the sun a little bit, and they have looong strings attached to the potatoes, the vine—looong strings. As soon as they lie in the sun they get like leather. So here's a black boy who's living in a chicken house on our place—living literally in a chicken house, working for, you know, five dollars a week. And we're the same age, you know, he's fifteen and I'm fifteen, that sorta thing. We talk about having *cars*, we talk about *girl*friends, we talk about going to *col*lege, we talk about *trav*eling, we talk about *clothes*. That's all we do, from morning to night, and that's the way that we lived. He eats in the kitchen at another table, from the same—my mother's cooking—that I do, that sorta thing, but he never eats with us, never lives in our house, never touches our water, y'know, he's completely segregated in every form and fashion. And I know very well he'll never go to school again, see, while I'm planning, of course, the whole career.

While we're doing this, we'd get in fights, you know, lots of fun, wrestling, you know, kill time. And in the process, we grabbed these leathery vines, like whips—leather whips, and started beating each other. See. Fourteen and fifteen years old. And, all in fun. And, and then all of a sudden, hit each other a little biting whip. And, and anger flares in both, both of us. And he's, he's bigger, and stronger, and can beat the hell out of me. And all of a sudden, he's raising like this (*he sits forward and arches his back, holding above his head an imaginary whip*) his whip that's gonna come down on me. And I'm down, and I can see it right now, I'm looking in his eyes, and he's full of hate, and to kill, and he's coming at me just with all his power (*he lifts his imaginary whip as if he'll strike*) and *just* as he does that, he stops.

(*He freezes. Intense, long pause.*)

And that moment I will *never* forget. And you tell me (*intense whisper*) *why* he stopped?

(*Pause.*)

Tell me *why* he stopped?

(*Pause.*)

He would have been killed. If I had cried and protested to anybody in that field, (*whispered*) *he* would have been the one punished. (*whispered slowly*) And he knew it and I knew it. And it dawned on me at that moment, the fight is unequal and it's unfair. It dawned on me at that moment that everything was gone. All our innocence was gone. Never again could we play. He realized it, and I realized it. It was *gone*. And it changed my life.

(*The names here, spoken by actors 2-6 will overlap: when one actor pronounces a last name, another actor begins a first name.*)

ACTOR 6: Clifford York

ACTOR 2: Nancy Attaway

ACTOR 5: Einar Michaelson

ACTOR 3: Mimi Thurman

ACTOR 4: Jack McClendon

ACTOR 6: Spencer Holloway

ACTOR 2: Jan Pew

ACTOR 5: Bill Landress

ACTOR 3: Carolyn Martin

ACTOR 4: Ben Weeks

ACTOR 6: Mac Lipsey

ACTOR 2: Carol Smith

ACTOR 5: Harris Mobley

ACTOR 3: Young prophets—

ACTOR 4: We wanted to change the world—

ACTOR 2: in thirty days or less—

ACTOR 5: For me Mercer was like a small flame—

ACTOR 3: a tiny, flickering flame —

ACTOR 8: that fanned into a consuming fire—

ACTOR 3: combustible

ACTOR 6: combustible

ACTOR 4: combustible

ACTOR 5: combustible

EVERYONE *(soft)*: burn.

(Beethoven's Moonlight Sonata, plays—the final notes of the piece. On a screen, the following is projected: "In 1956, Mac Bryan was barred from teaching a summer course co-sponsored by Mercer University. He had refused to stop talking about Martin Luther King in his ethics class. Later that year, he resigned from Mercer and took a job at Wake Forest University.")

Act II

"Man is a broken creature, yes; it is his nature as a human being to be so; but it is also his nature to create relationships that can span the brokenness."

—Lillian Smith
Killers of the Dream

Callings

ACTOR 6/STUDENT: Mac used to say it was fairly easy to teach church history, but to teach Christian ethics required living it.

ACTOR 2/STUDENT: I had a "taken-for granted" view of the world when I went to Mercer—

ACTOR 5/STUDENT: We had been so sheltered and lived in such a small world—

ACTOR 3/STUDENT: our comfortable little world—

ACTOR 4/STUDENT: he turned my life around—

ACTOR 6/STUDENT: stood my mind on end—

ACTOR 2/STUDENT: opened up the whole world to me—

ACTOR 4/STUDENT: the scales fell from my eyes in terms of social justice—

ACTOR 3/STUDENT: poverty—

ACTOR 5/STUDENT: racism—

ACTOR 6/STUDENT: we were a lot of truly idealistic people who thought somehow that we could make a big difference —

ACTOR 2/STUDENT: that we could bring in the Kingdom of God—

ACTOR 4/STUDENT: with advocacy—

ACTOR 3/STUDENT: with our very bodies—

ACTOR 6/STUDENT: like an underground railroad of friends across the South—

ACTOR 2/STUDENT: a very small group of radical people—

ACTOR 5/STUDENT: we could work it all out.

ACTOR 6/STUDENT: There was something—

ACTOR 2/STUDENT: something—

ACTOR 3/STUDENT: something—

ACTOR 6/STUDENT: that could be done.

ACTOR 5/STUDENT: *Combustible/Burn* eighth principle:

ACTOR 2/STUDENT: "We stand for the sense of Christian vocation—

ACTOR 4/STUDENT: in its deepest and widest implications."

ACTOR 6/STUDENT: Callings.

INCIDENT ON ROUTE 17

(*HARRIS MOBLEY, Mercer class of 1955, is very energetic, mischievous, and percolating with laughter—most of it derived at his own expense. He speaks in a crisp, deep, rough voice.*)

ACTOR 3/HARRIS MOBLEY: My father was a Deacon in a country church that my grandfather, his father, had helped organize in 1893. And I recall going in, gettin' the hell scared out of me on Sunday nights by rantin' and ravin' Baptist *(high voice)* preacher talkin' about the fiery hell and all that. And when I came to Savannah, I came of age and I didn't go to church. I never went back again.

(laughs) And then I had a spiritual experience.

It was 1951. I was an ignorant, country-boy, high-school dropout from Bethany, car-pooling home from Camp Legune, North Carolina with five drunken marines. And the kid driving had a brand new fifty-one Ford, and every beer, he'd go a little faster. And I was sittin' in the back seat with two guys, hittin' a few brews myself, raisin' hell on Route 17, everybody screamin', talkin', yellin', lyin', hollerin'—the driver's weavin' in and out of traffic—and I saw the speedometer hit a hundred and go past a hundred. And suddenly it occurred to me what was going to happen. We were going to have a mighty splash-up. There was no way out of this situation. *(laughs)*

And you know, I had one of those moments. I said to myself—I said "God save me and I'm yours." *(laughing)*

And no sooner than I had said that, to confirm this this ah…spiritual thing, this psychic phenomenon—whatever you want to call the damned thing—whatever it was— within thirty seconds, sixty seconds, there was a bloody accident up the road—and the— and the traffic slowed down. And we saw a decapitated lady. . . all of these people laying around the highway.

That slowed the driver down.

(Pause.)

It was just an accident as far as I'm concerned. I wouldn't want to cast it in a fundamentalist framework at all— *(ironic)* "Are you saved?"

But ah *(breathes out)*… I— I— I— I— just, you know, I felt that day in 1951 that I was no longer my own. I felt so many times I was pursuing a pledge—a promise I felt the need to fulfill. . . to something I couldn't see or didn't know anything about.

And I was always trying to keep my promise and never could. *(light laugh)* I could never get away from that, you know? It stayed with me.

It was like a bad dream.

(Pause.)

I was pursuing a promise when I resumed my education having been a high school dropout, enrolling at Mercer University, studying with a guy named Mac Bryan. If God ever spoke to me, it was through Mac (*laughs loud*). For some reason I was responsive to what he said. I ate it up. I just never turned back. I saw uh injustice as something that maybe we were made to live to correct, or address at least, whether we could ever correct it. *(laughs)*

One of Mac's favorite phrases was—(*impersonating Mac*) "don't talk to me about that flabby, flabby thing called love—

ACTOR 1/MAC BRYAN: —until you've dealt with that stern thing called justice."

ACTOR 3/HARRIS (*smiling*): He meant idle talk is easy for anybody. He was an action guy.

ACTOR 1/MAC BRYAN: Life is exciting. There's no such thing as being tired!

ACTOR 3/HARRIS MOBLEY *(he puts on a dashiki, an African covering)*: After I graduated from Mercer, I went to Africa, and Mac visited me there in November of 1959.

ACTOR 1/MAC BRYAN: He and I worked together and we came up with this scheme—

ACTOR 3/HARRIS MOBLEY: We were trying to break down the walls of segregation at Baptist universities—

ACTOR 1/MAC BRYAN: Since they wouldn't take black Americans, why not take one of their missionary products?

ACTOR 3/HARRIS MOBLEY: We were already considered those people who were "doing battle with cannibalism and darkness"— *(with irony)* had a certain "halo effect" for Baptist missionaries. The prevailing idea was that Africans live in trees. "Do you live in trees?" African students were actually asked that: do you live in trees? Tarzan.

Hilltop Christians

(SAM ONI, like MAC, is a theatrical presence—he sits forward in his chair, using his hands in precise and dramatic gestures, his deeply resonant and precise Anglo-African voice showing the most range of any character in the play, going from whispers to urgent shouts. He is a warm and open person and his voice registers this warmth. He wears khaki pants and a button-down shirt.)

ACTOR 9/SAM ONI: We were a colonial people. Ghana—well it was the Gold Coast then when I was born—fell under the colonial tutelage of the British. As I was growing up we were very poor. My father worked as a domestic for some British families. It *was* the context in which my own political consciousness began to be raised, because it suddenly struck me that in contrast to Ghanian culture—where the young minister to the needs of the old—the roles were reversed in my father's relation to these white people who were actually much younger than he was. Because whenever I would go to visit him, his master will call—

ACTOR 3/SAM ONI'S MASTER: *Daniel!*

ACTOR 9/SAM ONI: And you'd hear:

ACTOR 10/SAM ONI'S FATHER: *Yessuh!*

ACTOR 9/SAM ONI: You know, and my father would go running. And I thought that was odd.
    And then the agitation for independence began, and it was *then* that I was finally able to make the connection: so these white people, who have this privileged position for whom my father and others like my father were now subservient, didn't even *belong* among us! And I began to embrace the campaign, the agitation for an end to colonialism.
    In 1957 Ghana became independent—to great jubilation among Ghanians. Nkrumah's voice to this day still rings in my head—

ACTOR 10/NKRUMAH: *Ghana,* our mother land, is *free forever*!

ACTOR 9/SAM ONI: And we watched the Union Jack come down and the Ghanian flag go up. And it was a great moment. It was a great moment.
    And it was while I was working as a domestic myself that I met the first Southern Baptist missionary: Reverend and Mrs. McGuinness arrived. And being true to themselves and their own traditions in the American South, they chose to live where the former British colonial civil servants lived. It was an isolated suburb with fancy homes.

ACTOR 3/HARRIS MOBLEY: They were typical Southern Baptist missionaries with pith helmets and large Chevrolet station wagons, living up on the hill-top. The Europeans had just vacated it—thrown out of the country—but the missionaries had quickly captured *(laughs)* the hilltops.

ACTOR 9/SAM ONI: Well, I hit it off with David McGuinness, the son of the missionary couple. We became friends. And whenever I would walk over to David's house, the mother would see me coming and she would say—

ACTOR 4/MRS. MCGUINNESS (*patronizing but sugary*): Oh, you're here to see David.

ACTOR 9/SAM ONI: And I said "yes, madam."

ACTOR 4/MRS. MCGUINNESS: Ok wait here. *(she goes off-stage and calls out)* David! Sam is waiting to see you!

ACTOR 9/SAM ONI *(alone on stage)*: And so I was never invited into the house. Never invited into the house.

ACTOR 3/HARRIS MOBLEY: The Southern Baptists had simply transferred their sub-culture from the South and were trying to impose it *(laughs)* on *Africa!* It was *embarrassing.*

ACTOR 9/SAM ONI: Then the McGuinesses began inviting me to come to church with them. And when the white person begins to preach a sermon that promises a better life—it may not be in this lifetime, you know, but in the other dispensation—people were attracted. And then they asked me:

ACTOR 1/MR. MCGUINNESS *(as if to a child)*: Sam, do you know the Lord?

ACTOR 9/SAM ONI *(looking at the audience)*: And, you know, I've been a Christian all my life—I was born into an Anglican family—but they'd say:

ACTOR 1/MR. MCGUINNESS: Ohhhh, but that wasn't good enough.

ACTOR 9/SAM ONI: Ah, not good enough because the bap*tism* that I got as an Anglican wasn't going to *guarantee* a place for me in heaven *(chuckles once)*. None of this dab-dab-dab stuff *(dabs his forehead three times)*—the water on the forehead. You have to have a *to*tal immersion—that was the only sure way to make it to heaven. So I acquiesced.

(He is baptized by ACTOR 1.)

And I was Baptized. . . as a *Southern* Baptist.

The Land And The Gospel

ACTOR 3: From African critiques of missionary work in *The Missions on Trial*:

ACTOR 10/AFRICAN: The African in himself was of no interest to the missionary; he was of interest only in so far as he entered the Church and heartily joined in its work.

ACTOR 8/AFRICAN: The choice was accepting Christianity as a whole, just as it was presented, or receiving nothing.

ACTOR 7/AFRICAN: If we dance, we are excluded from the Church which the missionaries brought us.

ACTOR 10/AFRICAN: African religion was primarily life, power, center and meaning of life; now we have ended up in a net of commands and laws.

ACTOR 7/AFRICAN: The missionaries, as brothers of the white masters, diverted our attention from this world and turned it towards a heaven unconnected with this world.

ACTOR 8/AFRICAN: At first, we had the land and the white men had the Gospel.

ACTOR 10/AFRICAN: Then the missionaries came and taught us to close our eyes and say our prayers while the white men were stealing our land from us.

ACTOR 7/AFRICAN: And now we have the Gospel and they have the land.

ACTOR 9/SAM ONI: So this was their perspective—they had just gone filled with their own sense of self-importance as they'd gone to do these savages a favor. They lost out. They lost out.

Revelation

ACTOR 3/HARRIS MOBLEY: We met Sam in 1959. The missionaries had just thrown him out of the Baptist Secondary School in Kumatze for leading a protest of seventy students against a new exam schedule. They called him a rabble-rouser. *(smiling)* That only made me like him more.

ACTOR 9/SAM ONI: Harris Mobley's friendship was a bit more genuine, a bit more spontaneous than the other missionaries. We became friends almost on an equal footing—

ACTOR 3/HARRIS MOBLEY: We thoroughly enjoyed involving ourselves in the villages. Wonderful, liberating. . . after the diarrhea disappeared.

ACTOR 9/SAM ONI: In the late fifties, early sixties, the civil rights movement in the United States had been launched, eventually making headlines all over the world. And when I would read about demonstrations here, and freedom riders there, and confrontations with the police, I would turn to the missionaries—and most of them were very, very reluctant—in fact they were embarrassed, they didn't know how to deal with the question. Finally I turned to Harris.

ACTOR 3/HARRIS MOBLEY *(leveling with him)*: Sam, in America, in Georgia, where I'm from, if I were to take you with me to the church where I grew up, both of us would be turned away.

ACTOR 9/SAM ONI: Then he proceeded to tell me about other institutions of the Southern Baptists—their hospitals, their universities, their churches, every institution operated on a strictly segregated basis.

(Whispered, shocked even now.)

I *could* not believe it! I could not *believe* it! I could not reconcile the fact that the Southern Baptists, when they got the *inspiration* to embark on missionary work, of all the places they could have gone in the *world* (*soft but full*)... they chose the slave coast.

(Pause. Quiet.)

I was dumbfounded. It was a very disquieting revelation for me. And the more Harris and I talked about it, the more we felt a compelling need to do something to bring the Southern Baptists to see the contradiction in their tenets, in their preaching, and in their practice.

ACTOR 3/HARRIS MOBLEY: I started sending out letters of inquiry to Baptist universities back in the States.

ACTOR 9/SAM ONI: Of course, the response came, predictably one after the other, "thanks, but no thanks." Except for *Mercer* University.

ACTOR 3/HARRIS MOBLEY: I got a letter back from Rufus Harris, the President of Mercer University, telling me that the way to approach Sam's entry was to be in touch with John Mitchell, then Director of Admissions.

RUFUS HARRIS

ACTOR 2/JOHNNY MITCHELL *(friendly, bold and very confident)*: So I went up to President Rufus Harris's office, and I said "Dr. Harris, I haven't talked to you about ahh integration. I haven't talked to you about this before. Today I want to tell you that we have a student that I think is qualified. I want you to look at it."

ACTOR 1/RUFUS HARRIS *(imperiously looking at the application, in a high, seemingly aristocratic voice)*: What do you want to do?

ACTOR 2/JOHNNY MITCHELL: I want to take him.

ACTOR 1/RUFUS HARRIS: Ok Johnny, we'll take it to the trustees.

ACTOR 4: From the *Atlanta Journal*, July 23, 1962.

(Several actors reading newspapers on the stage.)

ACTOR 10: Mercer University President Rufus Harris says he will support integration before the trustees.

(An actor throws down a newspaper.)

And so far as he is concerned, their decision will be final.

(Another actor throws down a newspaper.)

Mercer is controlled to a large extent by the Georgia Baptist Convention. Should the trustees accept integration, Dr. Harris said he will then support its implementation *without reference to the convention.*

(Two actors throw down their newspapers and storm offstage.)

ACTORS 2, 4, AND 6: Rufus Harris.

ACTOR 2/JOHNNY MITCHELL: When Rufus Harris came to Mercer, he was sixty three years old. It was 1960, and he had a reputation as one of the greatest educators in the nation. Ask Mary Wilder over in the English Department about Rufus Harris—she'll tell you.

ACTOR 6/MARY WILDER: You gotta understand something: Dr. *Harris! Grrrrrrrrrrrr!* *(laughs)* You did *not* mess with Dr. Harris. He's been President of *Tu*lane, he's been *Dean* of the *law* school, he was back at Mercer—he'd *been* there, *done* that! You're *not* gonna *mess* with Harris! Ok? Have you talked to his secretary, Amelia Barclay? She'll tell you how it was.

ACTOR 4/AMELIA BARCLAY *(quiet and considerate)*: Trustees, Georgia Baptist Convention, ah, nothing, nothing fazed the man—

ACTOR 6/MARY WILDER *(interrupting her)*: When he decided something, that was the end of it. And he decided we were integrating, and we're not going to vote on it at the convention—that was the *end* of it! It was the *right thing*. Which I *looove*.

ACTOR 9/SAM ONI: I found out soon after that Mercer was willing to accept me, and I was more than eager to come. Well, word got out to the Georgia Baptist Convention, which controls Mercer University. . . and the whatchimicalit hits the fan.

ACTOR 10: Letters to the President of Mercer University:

ACTOR 5/LETTER-WRITER: Mercer was founded by *white* Georgia Baptists, operated and maintained by whites.

ACTOR 3/LETTER-WRITER: The student from Ghana is a *nigger* and will always be one and his admission naturally has to be refused.

ACTOR 4/LETTER-WRITER: Anyone that admits him should be *fired.*

ACTOR 3/LETTER-WRITER: The communists know that 25 years after they get these schools all mixed, then all races will be marrying, and in another 25 years, we will have a mixed weak-minded generation—

ACTOR 5/LETTER-WRITER: and they won't need to go to war to take this country, and then all creed of people, white and colored, will be their slaves.

ACTOR 3/LETTER-WRITER: Let's stop mixing schools and churches—this is treason!

ACTOR 4/AMELIA BARCLAY: President Harris had death threats—letters, phone calls, the works—usually country preachers or rabid segregationists. It was shocking.

ACTOR 2/JOHNNY MITCHELL: We tried to get him to close his blinds at night—

ACTOR 4/AMELIA BARCLAY: He always worked late in his office—

ACTOR 2/JOHNNY MITCHELL: We were sure somebody's gonna shoot him—

ACTOR 4/AMELIA BARCLAY: Everything *wide* open—anybody could walk down the street and see him in there—

ACTOR 2/JOHNNY MITCHELL: I said, "Dr. Harris, you sit up at that desk, I can see you from a block away. *(With sudden determination)* I'm telling you, we're going to close the blinds, you understand?"

ACTOR 4/AMELIA BARCLAY *(to HARRIS):* You know you shouldn't be doing this, let me close the blinds—

ACTOR 1/RUFUS HARRIS: No! Not *my* blinds! I'm going to leave them wide open.

ACTOR 4/AMELIA BARCLAY: That was the way he handled everything. I had never encountered that kind of personality.

ACTOR 6/MARY WILDER: This Baptist church wired him that they were going to withhold their money from Mercer. Rufus Harris figured out that their contribution to Mercer was sixty-seven cents. And so he writes them back that he was going to *personally* make up their part! *(bursts out laughing)* He was a character. He had more character than three characters put together!

ACTOR 4/AMELIA BARCLAY: He was the member of the largest Baptist church in New Orleans—totally different atmosphere from Georgia. And he just—he was, unprepared for the tirades that came his way. I mean we had thick files. And he said—

ACTOR 1/RUFUS HARRIS: You know, I never knew that Baptists could be so mean.

ACTOR 2/JOHNNY MITCHELL: I went to Atlanta, to the "Georgia Baptist Convention." And they introduced the Presidents of Shorter College, Tift College, Brewton Parker. And when they introduced Dr. Harris they booed him. All the preachers—now think about this—four or five hundred—when they introduced the greatest man, they booed him. And you know what? He acted like he didn't hear the boos.

ACTOR 1/RUFUS HARRIS *(Imperiously unfazed)*: Mitchell, I didn't hear any boos. Did you hear any boos?

ACTOR 2/JOHNNY MITCHELL: I said "yes I did, and I ain't goin to another convention. I'm not goin any more. 'Cause if those the ones who are leading us, they're the Christians? I must be in the wrong group."

Missionary in Reverse

ACTOR 10: Just days before the trustees were to vote on whether to admit Sam Oni to Mercer, Harris Mobley came to his alma mater to give a talk before chapel.

ACTOR 3/HARRIS MOBLEY: And the law school students had a protest as we were walking into that chapel—they were all out there with ugly signs: "Nigger-lover," "We don't want no niggers."

ACTOR 6/STUDENT: We have forced chapel, so it was kind of a ritualistic thing—a lot of days it was just people reading the papers and people milling around. But that day it was electric.

ACTOR 4/NARRATOR: From the 1963 speech:

ACTOR 3/HARRIS MOBLEY: Where do you find the missionary? Perched pretentiously on some imposing hilltop, isolated from the African community, in colonial fashion, high above the tin roofs of the villages below, or out in the exclusive suburb for Europeans.

ACTOR 1/LETTER-WRITER: We, the white citizens of Middle Georgia, are bitterly opposed to admission of negroes to Mercer University whether he or she be from Ghana or the United States.

ACTOR 3/HARRIS MOBLEY: Let the missionary mimic the colonial past. But let him also know he is thereby distorting the Christian Gospel—

ACTOR 5/LETTER-WRITER: I feel the good Lord made us different and religion doesn't have a thing to do with forcing us in our associates.

ACTOR 3/HARRIS MOBLEY: Christian compassion and racism will not mix; they are like oil and water.

ACTOR 2/LETTER-WRITER: A negro dancing with a white girl in a mixed school or mixed marriage, is the world's most—

ACTORS 2, 5, 1/LETTER-WRITERS: horrible crime against the Laws of God—

ACTOR 2/LETTER-WRITER: and anyone who teaches or preaches that this thing is right is your mortal enemy and is bound for Hell.

ACTOR 3/HARRIS MOBLEY: I would not ask any of you to go to the African or Asian mission field. You're in one here!

ACTORS 4/LETTER-WRITER: Integration is of the *devil!*

ACTOR 3/HARRIS MOBLEY: You don't need to go to Africa. You need to go home. Go to your homes and communities determined to demonstrate Christian brotherhood for God's sake.

ACTOR 2/LETTER-WRITER *(thundering)*: I will *never* contribute again to a Baptist school that is communized by mixing the races!

ACTORS 2, 5, 1/LETTER-WRITERS: *Never!*

ACTOR 6: From the *New York Times*, April 19:

ACTOR 10: Trustees of Mercer University today voted to admit students without regard to race. . . Mercer is the first Georgia institution to drop the traditional ban against admission of Negroes as students.

ACTOR 2/JOHNNY MITCHELL: Now keep this in mind. A great number of trustees resigned. A great number of trustees walked out. But they voted to take Sam.

ACTOR 4: From the *New York Herald Tribune* editorial, April 25:

ACTOR 10: Georgia's Mercer University, a Baptist institution, seems to have been the beneficiary of a little missionary work in reverse. Mr. Mobley went to Africa and converted Mr. Oni to Christianity. And now Mr. Oni has brought Mercer face to face with the "Christian ethic" of equality—and has converted the university.

ACTOR 3/HARRIS MOBLEY: Finally. For the first time, I felt like I was fulfilling a promise.

ACTOR 9/SAM ONI: And so, after waiting for an entire year, I arrived at Mercer in September, 1963, with my heart in my throat as Lemuel Penn, a black American GI, driving through Georgia, was shot to death.

Do-Gooders

ACTOR 1/DON BAXTER *(Mercer class of 1965. Eager, exuberant and enthusiastic, with a booming, confident voice)*: I went to Mercer to be a minister. When I was a junior at Mercer, I was just playing basketball. My whole life was tied up with studying, becoming a good student, making friends and being successful at basketball.

And then Harris Mobley came along and gave that talk. . . about the missionary coming down from their white houses into the valleys to take care of the natives and then going back up to their big white houses. And he said something about how we can't even deal with people who live across the street. After hearing Harris Mobley's speech, it dawned on me that I didn't have to spend my life getting ready to be a missionary to Africa—all I had to do was room with Sam Oni.

So I went to the housing meeting to try to work out the problem. I didn't want to be the one to take the, you know, take the burden. I thought some ministerial student or some, what I call "do-gooder," would do it. And nobody would do it. And finally, in a very indignant moment, I said "*I'll do* it! I'll room with him."

And that changed my life. That little statement, you know.

I was influenced by Harris Mobley just like he was by this Mac Bryan guy.

ACTOR 3/HARRIS MOBLEY *(smiling)*: See, so it works: Mac to me, me to Don.

ACTOR 1/DON BAXTER: There were things that happened. A guy I played basketball with used to get really furious and call me a "nigger-lover" and wouldn't throw me the ball in the basketball games. And we were on the same team. *(laughs)* I had a girlfriend that told me she didn't want to go out with me 'cause the girls in the sorority didn't think that would be a good idea because of Sam Oni. I wasn't in the social mainstream.

(Pause.)

In looking back I've always thought why did I do this, and did I do it for some ulterior motive, like did I want to be a do-gooder—did I want to get some points to go to heaven or something?
 I think it was more just human—that people need to be treated with justice.

GO BACK AND DREAM AGAIN

ACTOR 10/CARL BYAS: We used to tell a joke, when I was a kid, about the church over there: Vineville Baptist Church. Okay, so one morning, this black guy—John—goes to Vineville Baptist church. Sitting there. Person said:

ACTOR 3/WHITE MAN: Hey, what you want?

ACTOR 9/JOHN: I had a dream last night. The Almighty came to me in a dream, and told me to attend this church.

ACTOR 3/WHITE MAN: No, boy, you picked the *wrong dream.* You go back and dream—and dream again.

ACTOR 10/CARL BYAS *(chuckles)*: So about two or three Sundays passed and he came and told them the same thing:

ACTOR 9/JOHN: The Almighty came to me in a dream, and told me to attend this church.

ACTOR 3/WHITE MAN: No, boy, I told you already, you picked the wrong dream. You go back and dream again.

ACTOR 10/CARL BYAS: So all of a sudden, John, he didn't show up. So they started wondering, "Hey, what happened to John? What happened to John?" you know. So about four or five Sundays go outside and they see him:

ACTOR 3/WHITE MAN: Hey boy, come here. Did you have that dream again?

ACTOR 9/JOHN: Yeah, you folks were right. I had the dream. And the Almighty told me *He* been trying to get in this church for *forty years* and *He* hadn't made it—so I know *I* don't stand a chance!

(ACTOR 10/CARL BYAS laughs.)

Warm Welcome

ACTOR 1/DON BAXTER: Getting Sam Oni into a church, you see, was going to be our next big deal. So, I'm in my dormitory in the Fall—this is the first week that Sam Oni comes to the school. I'm with him, Sunday's coming up—and someone knocks on my door—

ACTOR 9/SAM ONI: Reverend Forrester, the minister of Tatnall Square Baptist Church. My very first Sunday—my very first weekend in Georgia, Reverend Forrester comes *marching* into our room in Sherwood Hall. Don Baxter and I roommates—

ACTOR 3/REV. FORRESTER *(very formal)*: Hello boys, how are you? I'm Reverend Forrester from Tatnall Square Baptist Church.

ACTOR 9/SAM ONI: Ah, well, nice to meet you. What can we do for you?

ACTOR 3/REV. FORRESTER: Don, can I talk to you outside?

ACTOR 1/DON BAXTER: I remember I walked out of the dormitory out there. There was a little bank of grass and I stood on that bank. And I remember the sun was starting to go down. It was sunset. And he came up very formally—he had a full suit on with a tie— and he said—

ACTOR 3/REV. FORRESTER *(nervous, polite)*: I need to talk to you. You know, you're certainly welcome in our church—but I just have to tell you, Sam Oni is not welcome at our church. And if he comes he will be arrested.

(Pause. DON looks at FORRESTER.)

ACTOR 1/DON BAXTER: I just. . . quietly sat there, looking at a person that that. . . I just couldn't quite comprehend. I looked at him a minute, I remember, and I said "ok, I'm glad to know. Thanks for giving me that information."
And after this episode with the church at Tatnall Square, I decided I didn't want to be a minister. That's when organized religion kind of lost me. That was the most powerful sermon I ever got in a negative way. After that, I decided that I was going to medical school.

ACTOR 9/SAM ONI: Don had made up his mind with me that the place to worship was not going to be Tatnall Square Baptist Church but rather Vineville Baptist Church.

ACTOR 1/DON BAXTER: It was either that day or the next day I got a call from the Vineville church, and it was a Dr. Walter Moore. He said—

ACTOR 2/MOORE: Don, why don't you bring Sam Oni to our church? I *think* he will be allowed to worship with us.

ACTOR 1/DON BAXTER: "I think," is what he said. And I said "thank you very much I'll do that." I took Sam. We're going up the street in my car—

ACTOR 9/SAM ONI: —headed toward sanctuary for worship

ACTOR 1/DON BAXTER: It's tense. We're both tense.

ACTOR 9/SAM ONI: I probably shouldn't have gone—

ACTOR 1/DON BAXTER: We walk into the church—

ACTOR 4/CHURCH MEMBER: That church was packed, and nobody moved—

ACTOR 1/DON BAXTER: You can feel the heaviness in the whole place. Walter Moore was preaching—

ACTOR 9/SAM ONI: And at the end of the sermon, Reverend Moore, as is the practice in Southern Baptist Churches—

ACTOR 1/DON BAXTER: He asked for people to come forward—

ACTOR 9/SAM ONI: So everybody gets up—

ACTOR 1/DON BAXTER: and the two of us came down—

ACTOR 9/SAM ONI: with about a dozen other students. And then you line up to face the congregation. And it usually is a formality: they usually greet you and they welcome and you go back to your seats.

ACTOR 2/WALTER MOORE: Well, because this is a little different, why don't we vote on this group first?

ACTOR 1/DON BAXTER: So they took all of the—all of us whites, pulled us over, and of course everybody voted yes. And then—

ACTOR 9/SAM ONI: Reverend Moore said to everybody to go back and sit down except for *me*.

ACTOR 2/WALTER MOORE: Well, we're very privileged, we're very blessed to have in our midst this morning Sam Oni, a young man who came to know the Lord through our missionary efforts in Africa.

ACTOR 9/SAM ONI: —and before he could finish that sentence, one man was on his feet.

ACTOR 3/OBJECTOR: Reverend Moore I am *not* going to sit here and watch you destroy this church by bringing niggers into the congregation!

ACTOR 9/SAM ONI: All red-faced—and he went on and on and on. Before he was done, another woman was up.

ACTOR 4/OBJECTOR: *My* grandfather helped found this church and I'm not going to allow you to bring niggers into the congregation!

ACTOR 1/DON BAXTER: Well, I'm just standing there and I can't believe this is taking place—

ACTOR 9/SAM ONI: —another man was up on his feet. At which point, after the third man finished his ranting and raving, Reverend Moore said "let's put the matter to a vote."

ACTOR 2/WALTER MOORE: Those in favor of Sam Oni's membership please raise your hands.

ACTOR 9/SAM ONI: The hands went up—

ACTOR 2/WALTER MOORE: Those opposed please raise your hands—

ACTOR 4/CHURCH MEMBER: There was a sizable vote against Sam being admitted—

ACTOR 9/SAM ONI: But I could tell, the minister could tell, a slim majority favored my membership. But the die-hards won't give up. So they took the vote the *second* time. They *still* won't give up. So Reverend Moore then said to them—

ACTOR 2/WALTER MOORE: Let's do a standing vote.

ACTOR 1/DON BAXTER: The vote was not overwhelmingly for him, but it was enough. He was voted in.

ACTOR 9/SAM ONI: And that was how I was *so warmly welcomed,* my very first Sunday, into the house of God to worship in America—the home base of the missionaries who've been coming to my part of the world for a hundred and thirteen years. My *first Sunday!*

ACTOR 8: From the Associated Press

ACTOR 10: A 2000-member baptist Church accepted a ministerial student from Takoradi, Ghana Sunday and became the first Baptist Church in Georgia to desegregate its membership.

ACTOR 5: From the *Atlanta Constitution*:

ACTOR 6 *(triumphant)*: The light that shines from the story dispels some of the darkness of a troubled world. . . The congregation voted unanimously to accept Mr. Oni.

EVERYONE: *What?*

ACTOR 6 *(very proud)*: The action of the Vineville church, we believe, represents the kind of vitality that has kept the Christian church alive for nearly 2,000 years.

ACTOR 1/DON BAXTER: I was just so. . . amazed. . . that Sam Oni was voted into a white Baptist church—that I got him in without getting arrested. So it was a victory. That church did something that gives them a star to this day.

(Pause.)

And yet, it was another nail in my coffin about becoming part of organized religion. Because I somehow thought that when people went to church, they—they were Christian and they did the Christian thing. I just lost some of the idealism and some of the desire to dedicate my life to something where I was going to have fifty percent of the people voting against what was right.

ACTOR 9/SAM ONI: That day was the beginning of a four-year faith-shattering experience. My coming should have been a non-*event!* God says, "in this fine woman here *(points to someone in the audience)* this woman is a part of me and I am a part of her." So I have no choice in deciding whether to accept or not to accept her. It was so *simple*: the faith is the leavening influence that helps me to finally recognize that this man, my brother, *(urgently whispered)* we're children of the same God.

ACTOR 1/DON BAXTER: Driving home I said "Sam," I said, "why do you think I got more votes than you did?" (*laughing*) And he said—

ACTOR 9/SAM ONI: Because you're taller.

ACTOR 1/DON BAXTER: Don't you love that?

Mary and Betty

(*MARY WILDER, Mercer class 1954, Mercer Professor of English, 1957-1998. Mary has a pointed and clipped mountain accent occasionally punctuated by a smoker's cough. She's feisty, forthright, hilarious and gloriously foul-mouthed. She'd later be one of the preeminent feminists on campus, a playwright, and the first woman to run for Mayor of Macon.*)

ACTOR 6/MARY WILDER: I was there. At Vineville Baptist. I didn't want *any* kind of voting *any*where on *any*body. . . could come or not come to a church! Christ didn't *vote* on who could be in or out. You don't *vote*! Period. Jesus was a revolutionary, and a civil- rightser, and a feminist, and a—(*sensing possible opposition*) sure he was! If I thought that the New Testament and Christianity was all about the submission of women, I wouldn't be a Christian. All this that people come up with about women in their place: that's bullshit. Show me that! Show me where Christ *ever* put *any*body in their "place." (*barely audible*) No. (*louder and higher*) Noo. (*lower pitch*) Noo. (*lowest and final, leaving no doubt*) No.

(*Pause.*)

It was in 1963—the year Sam Oni came to Mercer—that I had my eyes opened about women. I read *The Feminine Mystique*. Just as the whole Civil Rights movement brought to my attention the injustices done to blacks, the *Feminine Mystique* brought to my attention that women were shuffled into teaching, and nursing, and all the "women's" careers, not doctor, lawyer, and Indian chief. Growing up, it never occurred to me that I could be anything but a teacher or a nurse. I mean, I might have gone into science or math. I was taught those subjects were "out of women's reach." Business? Law? Medicine? Forget it.

ACTOR 4: From *The Feminine Mystique*, by Betty Friedan:

ACTOR 5: Women learned that truly feminine women do not want careers, higher education, political rights.

ACTOR 4: They were taught to pity the neurotic, unfeminine, unhappy women who wanted to be poets or physicists or presidents.

ACTOR 5: All they had to do was devote their lives from earliest girlhood to finding a husband and bearing children.

ACTOR 4: The problem lay buried, unspoken, for many years in the minds of American women.

ACTOR 6/MARY WILDER: I taught at Mercer when there was not one woman in the law school, because they didn't accept women's applications. There were no women sports teams: if you played sports, it'd mess up your menstruation and you wouldn't have babies. It would hurt baby-making, see. You had to put on raincoats over your shorts when you went to the gym. And it never occurred to us to protest our situation at Mercer. Never. It never did. Wearing those raincoats was like wearing a veil. Until the Civil Rights movement, we did not begin to look at our *own* civil rights, see.

ACTOR 5/BETTY FRIEDAN: This is not what being a woman means, no matter what the experts say . . . Only when women are permitted to use their full strength, to grow to their full capacities, can the feminine mystique be shattered.

ACTOR 6/MARY WILDER: Here's a children's game: Red Rover, Red Rover. Alright. You have two sides, and everybody's holding hands, and you get these real grips. And you say "Red Rover, Red Rover, send Mary over." So, Mary has to run at you, and break somebody's hold. You have to run through the line. And you do that until one side has everybody. But see if you *run*, and you jump at the last minute, and raise your knee to these arms, *(leaning forward)* you can break them.

Eleven Ways of Looking at a Black Girl

(In the following scenes, three actors play one woman—SAMARIA "COOKIE" MITCHUM. Actor 8 recollects her younger self: actor 7 plays YOUNG COOKIE at age twelve and actor 10 plays TEENAGE COOKIE at age 17. The changes in this scene should move quickly and without much pause. SAMARIA "COOKIE" MITCHUM's voice is an amalgam of different characteristics: tough, vulnerable, and friendly. She has the most intense, unrestrained, joyous laughter.)

I.

ACTOR 8/SAMARIA "COOKIE" MITCHUM: My family lived in East Macon, where the Coliseum is now—near the Ocmulgee river—and the water, when it really rained, it would come up near our street.

ACTOR 7/YOUNG "COOKIE" MITCHUM: They call us river-rats.

II.

ACTOR 8/SAMARIA "COOKIE" MITCHUM *(referring to ACTOR 7)*: This is me at age twelve:

ACTOR 7/YOUNG "COOKIE" MITCHUM *(pantomiming scrubbing a floor)*: My mother is a maid. We help her clean—help her scrub the floors, tile floors, on our hands and knees. One time, I was working for my mother in one of her jobs, and I hurt my back and I couldn't get up. And my mother took me to a doctor, and the doctor told her:

ACTOR 2/DOCTOR: Well Annie May, if you'd make these children get off of their lazy butts and work—that's what's wrong with her, she's *lazy*—she's not using her muscles.

ACTOR 8/SAMARIA "COOKIE" MITCHUM: Momma said, *(quiet but intense)* "Dr. Bertsom, she was scrubbing the floor when she got this cramp in her back."

ACTOR 7/YOUNG "COOKIE" MITCHUM: I will not think about these things until I am a grown woman. And then it will make me angry.

III.

ACTOR 8/SAMARIA "COOKIE" MITCHUM: My parents—oh my Lord—they worked so hard to make sure that all ten of us were educated—

ACTOR 7/YOUNG "COOKIE" MITCHUM: We go to church every day, twice on Sundays. We walk to the black library every Saturday—and we walk back home. And if we miss, we get a spanking. And if we say it looks like it's going to rain, and that's the reason we can't go—

(Pause, looks up at the sky uncertainly, then to the audience.)

we better hope it rains.

IV.

ACTOR 8/SAMARIA "COOKIE" MITCHUM: We also go to music lessons once a week—

ACTOR 7/YOUNG "COOKIE" MITCHUM: I get my piano lessons with my piano teacher who is blind. My piano teacher is named Pinky Wilder. She was in school with Ray Charles.

(They play.)

And now a lot of times I play with my eyes closed.

V.

(ACTOR 10 begins furiously miming writing, occasionally looking at her watch. ACTOR 6 passes by to check that she's not cheating.)

ACTOR 8/SAMARIA "COOKIE" MITCHUM *(regarding actor 10 at work)*: This is me in 1964 at age seventeen. That year the first schools in Macon integrated—

ACTOR 10/TEENAGE "COOKIE" MITCHUM: I am a senior, a straight-A student in the black high school. They bring all of us into Mercer to be tested before we integrate the school system, and give us reading comprehension tests to see who will most likely make it in the white schools—

ACTOR 8/SAMARIA "COOKIE" MITCHUM: Every book we were ever given in our schools had another white school stamped in there—we got all of the old books.

ACTOR 10/TEENAGE "COOKIE" MITCHUM: While I'm taking the test, I hear the white lady who administered them saying:

ACTOR 6/WHITE ADMINISTRATOR: Ahh, these kids can't read. They've got them fooled over there at that school thinking that they're A students.

ACTOR 10/TEENAGE COOKIE MITCHUM: Like it was no big deal whether we hear it or not!

ACTOR 8/SAMARIA "COOKIE" MITCHUM: I'm fifty four years old and I still remember that.

ACTOR 10/TEENAGE "COOKIE" MITCHUM: That was one of the main reasons I volunteered to integrate. I wanted to see if I was as bright as they said I was. I wanted to see if I could make it.

VI.

ACTOR 8/SAMARIA "COOKIE" MITCHUM: Nobody knew what was going to happen that first day of school in 1964, the first year of integration in the city of Macon. The police escorted us.

(ACTOR 10 approaches ACTOR 5/WHITE TEACHER, sitting at a desk.)

ACTOR 10/TEENAGE "COOKIE" MITCHUM: When I went to Miller that day as one of seven black students integrating an all white girl's school, they told me—

ACTOR 5/WHITE TEACHER *(looking down at her list)*: Well we have too many of you. You need to go down to Dudley Hughes Vocational School.

(ACTOR 10 walks to the other side of the stage, where ACTOR 9/ BILL RANDALL sits.)

ACTOR 8/SAMARIA "COOKIE" MITCHUM: And I'll never forget walking all the way over to Bill Randall's office—Bill Randall was a civil rights activist in Macon who helped get Miller integrated—I said:

ACTOR 10/TEENAGE "COOKIE" MITCHUM: Mr. Randall, they told me that they had too many of us already, but I don't want to go to the vocational school because I want to go to college.

ACTOR 8/SAMARIA "COOKIE" MITCHUM: And he said:

ACTOR 9/JUDGE BILL RANDALL: Baby, you walk *right back* over there and you go on to class.

(ACTOR 10 once again traverses the stage to go back to school.)

ACTOR 8/SAMARIA "COOKIE" MITCHUM: I said "yes sir."

ACTOR 10/TEENAGE "COOKIE" MITCHUM: So now I'm walking back over there to go back to class. *(Pause, to the audience)* I am *so tired* of walking.

VII.

ACTOR 8/SAMARIA "COOKIE" MITCHUM: When I was a senior in high school, a group of us girls had a singing group. We called ourselves.

ACTORS 7, 8, AND 10: The Bojelles

(ACTORS 7, 8 AND 10 join each other as the singing group)

ACTOR 7/A BOJELLE: We all had four part harmony

ACTOR 10/A BOJELLE: We wrote our own music

ACTOR 8/SAMARIA "COOKIE" MITCHUM: We choreographed our own dance steps.

(They show the audience a quick dance move.)

ACTOR 10/TEENAGE "COOKIE" MITCHUM: The white girls at Miller—those girls were crazy. They already had placed me as a star. They would write things in my yearbook like—

ACTOR 5/HIGH SCHOOL GIRL: Don't forget us when you make it big time!

ACTOR 6/HIGH SCHOOL GIRL: Remember us when you're in Hollywood!

ACTOR 10/TEENAGE "COOKIE" MITCHUM: One day, we had that whole gym—girls and guys—standing up *screaming* as if we had already been to the mountaintop. (*Laughs.*)

(Sound of cheers.)

VIII.

ACTOR 8/SAMARIA "COOKIE" MITCHUM: A few days after that concert—

ACTOR 10/TEENAGE "COOKIE" MITCHUM: I'm in the cafeteria, and somebody takes the cap off the milk and throws it at me. *(flinching as if hit with something)* And hits me in the back with it.

ACTOR 8/SAMARIA "COOKIE" MITCHUM: And I looked at my friend, and I said:

ACTOR 10/TEENAGE "COOKIE" MITCHUM *(very tough)*: Now, I'm *not* going to turn around to see who threw that cap. Because if I do, *both* of us will end up in jail.

ACTOR 8/SAMARIA "COOKIE" MITCHUM: So it doesn't matter about the singing. They love the music, but they don't love *you*.

IX.

ACTOR 10/TEENAGE "COOKIE" MITCHUM: It is later that year and I am trying to apply to Mercer and my guidance counselor is calling my mom to let her know that I'm being—

ACTOR 4/GUIDANCE COUNSELOR *(dialing, very annoyed)*: Uncooperative, obstinate, disrespectful—

ACTOR 10/TEENAGE "COOKIE" MITCHUM: I am a senior—I have a little bit more *guts*. This is one time I will not agree and just keep my mouth closed and go along with the program.

ACTOR 4/GUIDANCE COUNSELOR: Hello, Mrs. Mitchum—

ACTOR 8/SAMARIA "COOKIE" MITCHUM: And they put my mother on the phone with me, and she said, "Cookie what is the matter?"

ACTOR 10/TEENAGE "COOKIE" MITCHUM: The counselor refuses to write a recommendation to the college of my choice. She's willing to grant me scholarships to—

ACTOR 4/GUIDANCE COUNSELOR *(suddenly encouraging)*:
Savannah State, Fort Valley State and Albany State—

ACTOR 8/SAMARIA "COOKIE" MITCHUM: All black schools—

ACTOR 10/TEENAGE "COOKIE" MITCHUM: But they told me that I'm not good enough to go to Mercer.

ACTOR 8/SAMARIA "COOKIE" MITCHUM: My parents didn't want us kids getting involved in any kind of conflicts. So I was surprised when my mother said, "Cookie I'm behind you. I'm behind you one hundred percent."

ACTOR 4/GUIDANCE COUNSELOR: We're not going to disgrace ourselves by sending her over to Mercer with SAT scores as low as she has. *(hanging up and turning to ACTOR 10)* You'll never make it.

ACTOR 10/TEENAGE "COOKIE" MITCHUM: All of the other seniors—whites—went wherever they told them they'd go, but the seven of us who had integrated that school, they wouldn't let any of us apply to Mercer. I tell her I don't need her help. I'll get into Mercer on my own.

X.

ACTOR 8/SAMARIA "COOKIE" MITCHUM: When I got back home, I called the admissions office of Mercer University and I wouldn't let the man off the phone until they let me talk to someone about this.

ACTOR 10/TEENAGE "COOKIE" MITCHUM *(speaking on the phone)*: If I send in an application, you'll turn it down. You need to see me. You need to hear my voice. The application is not *me*.

ACTOR 8/SAMARIA "COOKIE" MITCHUM: So they set up a meeting with the Dean of Students, Joe Hendricks.

ACTOR 10/TEENAGE "COOKIE" MITCHUM: And I tell him, "I don't care what those scores say, I *know* that I can do this work if I'm given the chance."

ACTOR 8/SAMARIA "COOKIE" MITCHUM: Dean Hendricks said:

ACTOR 2/JOE HENDRICKS: It's hard to accept students not recommended by their schools. . . We'll give y'all a chance. We're going to let you take a summer school course. Now if you don't pass, you can't come in.

ACTOR 10/TEENAGE "COOKIE" MITCHUM: I said "I'm going to pass that course."

XI.

ACTOR 8/SAMARIA "COOKIE" MITCHUM: My name is Samaria Mitchum—

ACTOR 7/YOUNG "COOKIE" MITCHUM: My friends call me "Cookie."

ACTOR 10/TEENAGE "COOKIE" MITCHUM: They said I wasn't smart enough.

ACTOR 7/YOUNG "COOKIE" MITCHUM: Disrespectful—

ACTOR 10/TEENAGE "COOKIE" MITCHUM: I wasn't going to make it.

(ACTORS 7, 8 AND 10 join hands.)

ACTOR 8/SAMARIA "COOKIE" MITCHUM: In 1965, I enrolled at Mercer University.

The Invisible

ACTOR 7/ERNESTINE COLE: My parents dropped me off at Mercer and I felt very alone. And that feeling *intensified* during the course of the next three years.

ACTOR 8/BETTY J. WALKER: The students, they just kind of ignored us. We were like invisible—you know, like the Invisible Man.

ACTOR 9/GARY JOHNSON: The only amount of communication we had with our white colleagues was scribbling on the bathroom walls, and that was usually about some kind of sexual mythology. Oh they thought that black men were ah these sexual *giants*, you know, and definitely wanted to *rape* white women and it was just—(*in disgust*) ughhh. I mean it was primitive. They didn't have a *clue* as to who we were.

ACTOR 10/LYDIA DUMAS: You had them coming out of the country, and they would believe stupid things like, "Do you bleed red?" They felt that they had the right to come in my room, pretending to see my roommate, and I noticed they kept hanging around until midnight. I was wondering what the heck was wrong with them. One girl was from Winder, Georgia, and had been taught that black people grew tails after midnight. She was serious. She actually believed that bull! I threw her butt out of my room.

ACTOR 9/GARY JOHNSON I had an English class in Willingham Chapel. I was the only black student in that class. And ah, I sat down, and the students filter in, and nobody sits near me.

(Pause.)

Nobody sits in my row. The *entire* class sat behind me. And so that is a picture that ah (*short pause*) I—I could never forget. I remember I called mother the first week I was there, and I told her, "I'm coming home, this is crazy, this doesn't make any sense." It was, it was just—I don't know.

(Pause.)

You thought you had gone to hell.

ACTOR 7/ERNESTINE COLE: I tell you my biggest realization and probably my lowest moment. . . was when ah—I was walking across the campus one day, I was going back to my dormitory, coming from class. I was on the sidewalk, and I was just walking, minding my business, right in front of Porter Hall. And a group of white boys passed by and spit at me. And some of it. . . some of the film. . . touched my body.

(Pause.)

I was in a pensive mood and I didn't expect that. And they brought me back I guess. . . to reality. . . in Macon, Georgia. . . at that time. And I felt angry, and I felt, you know, where am I? What is this? And why am I here, if I have to be taunted with insults such as this?

(Pause.)

No. I felt very low at that point.

PAPA JOE

ACTOR 10/STUDENT: Joseph Hendricks, Dean of Students, recruited me for Mercer—

ACTOR 9/STUDENT: He was a country boy—no airs—

ACTOR 8/STUDENT: Joe came to my high school—

ACTOR 10/STUDENT: Met with my guidance counselor—

ACTOR 7/STUDENT: Very few colleges in Georgia were recruiting African Americans like this—

ACTOR 8/STUDENT: He came up with a way to get us in there—

ACTOR 10/STUDENT: And then he protected us after we got there.

ACTOR 9/STUDENT: He had us doing *everything*, and anything we wanted to do, he wanted us to do it.

ACTOR 7/STUDENT: He was a different kind of radical. He was a subtle radical.

ACTOR 8/STUDENT: Dr. Hendricks was sort of like an *enzyme*. *(laughs hard)* He's something that makes things happen without himself being absorbed or destroyed.

ACTOR 7/STUDENT: He was our number one advocate and kind of considered us his children.

ACTOR 8/STUDENT: He makes the reaction go!

ACTOR 10/STUDENT *(laughing)*: He was our big white daddy.

ACTORS 7-10: Papa Joe.

ACTOR 2/JOE HENDRICKS: When I was a kid in Talbot County, I never gave any thought to segregation. Going to school, I'd be standing out in the freezing cold—and blacks were walking down the road, and we were getting on the school bus and driving. And black kids walking miles—teachers walking with them to that one room school. Seven grades for the black schools. Seven grades taught by one teacher. Shut down whenever we had to shake the peanuts, pick the cotton. They stayed out to plant our crops. And my father was chairman of the school board. I never saw nothin' wrong with it. "This is the way the world is." Never any questions.

(Pause)

I think my real awakening was right there in Groover Hall as an undergraduate at Mercer University, in a class with one of my liberators: Mac Bryan. If there ever was a prophetic teacher he was one.

ACTOR 1/MAC BRYAN: You ask, "what is a prophet?" A prophet is a nobody coming from the woods. See, the prophet doesn't have to have a tradition. Amos says, "I'm a nobody. I came from the woods. I have no village. I have no degrees. I speak. Who do I speak for? Yahweh."

ACTOR 2/JOE HENDRICKS: Now Mac was punching the elephant's butt—the elephant being segregation—running at issues like a locomotive. And he's feelin that he has the responsibility to suffer in this process.

ACTOR 1/MAC BRYAN: The prophet must go to the people he's prophesied against, he must live with those people, and suffer with them, and he must die with them. It's a hard road, brother. That's why they're barefooted.

ACTOR 2/JOE HENDRICKS *(smiling at this)*: Mac Bryan is just a much more moral man than I am (*chuckles*). Mac tells you what he's going to do. It's sort of a prophetic notion—he puts it out there.

ACTOR 1/MAC BRYAN: You've got to make them wrestle with their conscience!

ACTOR 2/JOE HENDRICKS: And then the other people like me, you know, my notion is tell any lie you need to get the job done. Do whatever you need to do to get blacks in Mercer. It calls for swivel hips. I mean, you don't run straight into the line.

ACTOR 1/MAC BRYAN: When the social structure comes to a breaking point, you *have* to cross over that line.

ACTOR 2/ JOE HENDRICKS: You have to think about what you're trying to do. Are you trying to witness or are you trying to achieve an end?

ACTOR 1/MAC BRYAN: You have to choose sides. You have to move sometime! See, so you're going, see you're going, you're leaping, you're leaping out, you're taking risks!

ACTOR 2/ JOE HENDRICKS *(Looks at him, smiling)*: Mac and I differ completely in the way we look at the world, but I would never have ended up doing what I was doing as Dean of Students at Mercer if it hadn't been for Mac Bryan.

(Pause.)

It's when the prophets grow quiet that you need to get worried.

Skin

ACTOR 10: What color's that?

ACTOR 5: That's white

ACTOR 10: What color's that?

ACTOR 5: Black.

ACTOR 10 *(looking at her closely)*: You ever see any people either one of those damn colors?

EVERYONE: Skin.

ACTOR 8/STUDENT: There were all sorts of schisms in the black community. There was Sam Oni: Sam was not really part of that black community. He was an African.

ACTOR 9/SAM ONI: I came from Africa with *supreme* self confidence, borne of the fact that I as an African man grew up among Africans who never stopped for a moment to wonder about their *"Africanness."* Do you wake up and say, "oh God, I'm oh *sooo* glad that I'm white! And my nose is a little pointy and, you know." No! As far as I was concerned, I'm fine. Ain't nothing wrong with *me*. I was comfortable in my own skin.

ACTOR 7/STUDENT: We didn't *hate* him, we just—he was treated differently, and he acted differently, and he actually *was* different, you know: he hadn't gone through the black American experience. He didn't see himself like we saw ourselves, and we had a lot of re-thinking to do as far as conceptualizing of ourselves as human beings and first class citizens. But Sam never obviously had to do that. He's probably always been a first-class citizen in his country.

ACTOR 10/STUDENT: The only similarity was the color of our skin. You know, and I felt sorry for him, but he didn't seem like he wanted us to befriend him. But he was probably lonesome, and he was being mistreated. His *entire* world was crushed when he found out that the people who brought him over here did not accept him as a human being.

ACTOR 9/SAM ONI: I sort of slept-walked my way through it—through those years. The racism nearly broke my spirit.

(Pause. Looks away. Exhales.)

But, the resilience is there and we—we survive and we are able to go on. But eh, the worst part of it— of those four horrendous years, was my mother's death.

(Pause.)

I'll tell you how it happened. I completed my first year and I was *seriously* having second thoughts. . . whether I should. . . stick with this. I knew for sure I had bitten off more than I could chew. So one hot summer day. . . I was in my room. Dr. Otto called and said he would like to see me in his office.

ACTOR 3/BOB OTTO: Sam, as your Christian brother, I have a very sad duty to perform.

ACTOR 9/SAM ONI: He reached into his shirt pocket, and pulled out an air-o-gram.

ACTOR 3/BOB OTTO: I have just received this letter from your country. From your older brother. It announces the death of your mother.

ACTOR 9/SAM ONI: All I remember was just collapsing into a heap. I just didn't think it was right or fair for—for me never to set eye on that woman again. For me never... for me never to let her glory and...

(Pause.)

I was the first in my family to go to get a college education. Yah. Em, for me not to go show off and for her to glory in the fact that eh, "that's my boy."

(Very long pause. Again, looking away. Breathing in, through tears. Finally breathing out.)

Yah.

THE MIRROR

ACTOR 10/STUDENT: Mercer had a reputation of being a great school in addition to the fact that it was religious. And its religious base had *a lot* to do with what happened to us—and what happened also in terms of the blacks and whites eventually coming together in some kind of way.

ACTOR 5/STUDENT: I went to Mercer that first year and *just* had my eyes opened with everything!

ACTOR 1/STUDENT: Those first years were just a sea change for me in every way.

ACTOR 7/STUDENT: Young black folks at the time, church was just something that you grew up with. . . it had been sort of a blind faith type thing. But Mercer made it a search.

ACTOR 5/STUDENT: I began to learn that there was more than one way of looking at things—

ACTOR 1/STUDENT: That famous saying in the 25th chapter of Matthew—

ACTOR 7/STUDENT: "In as much as you have done unto the least, you have done unto me."

ACTOR 1/STUDENT: I mean, that's a powerful statement.

ACTOR 3/STUDENT: We are called to see Christ in everybody who suffers—that He is suffering in them. And we have a responsibility to respond—

ACTOR 10/STUDENT: And we basically had whites crossing that line because I think that their consciences began to mess with them.

ACTOR 6/STUDENT: "In as much as you have done unto the least—

ACTOR 5/STUDENT: least—

ACTOR 7/STUDENT: least—

ACTOR 8/STUDENT: you have done unto me."

ACTOR 1/STUDENT: me—

ACTOR 4/STUDENT: me—

ACTOR 5/STUDENT: me—

ACTOR 10/STUDENT: me.

ACTOR 3/STUDENT: When you are an instrument of injustice or whenever you are *complicit* with injustice against—

ACTOR 10/STUDENT: people on the margins—

ACTOR 6/STUDENT: then you have done that very act of injustice to God, God's self.

ACTOR 10/STUDENT: The Civil Rights movement I think really used that as a mirror, basically saying—

ACTOR 8/STUDENT: This is you—look at yourself.

ACTOR 7/STUDENT: How is it that you call yourself a Christian, acting like that?

ACTOR 5/STUDENT: "Neither Jew nor Gentile—

ACTOR 10/STUDENT: slave nor free—

ACTOR 6/STUDENT: male nor female"—

ACTOR 8/STUDENT: Jesus was for justice for all.

ACTOR 4/STUDENT: Meaning the kingdom of God is here—

ACTOR 7/STUDENT: here—

ACTOR 9/STUDENT: here—

ACTOR 3/STUDENT: here—

ACTOR 2/STUDENT: It's inaugurated. It's among us—

ACTOR 6/STUDENT: My search had begun.

Gospel Music Seminar

ACTOR 8/STUDENT: Deep in his heart Dean Hendricks really wanted to *push* the integration process at Mercer.

ACTOR 3/ED BACON (*Class of 1968. ED speaks deliberately, softly relishing words when he gets to a memory that he loves*): I helped Joe and some others develop a Sunday night gathering in the cafeteria of black and white students for singing and prayer. Cookie Mitchum and I were a team.

ACTOR 8/SAMARIA "COOKIE" MITCHUM: We would have these evenings we would spend and sing—

ACTOR 3/ED BACON: Cookie would play the piano—

ACTOR 8/SAMARIA "COOKIE" MITCHUM: And Ed would lead the singing. And we spent a lot of Sunday afternoons like that—

ACTOR 3/ED BACON: And we would be in ecstasy for about fifteen to thirty minutes singing through all the songs—

ACTOR 8/SAMARIA "COOKIE" MITCHUM: I'll never forget: Ed Bacon and I went to a retreat, and he wanted me to play some hymn or something. Well, I was brought up as a Southern Baptist, and there are some songs that are written in the hymn books when I was growing up, we put more *feeling* and, you know, slow it down and kinda jazz it up a little bit. We put a lot of beat and rhythm to it. I think the song was "Amazing Grace." Well, Ed was up there trying to (*laugh*) *direct* the hymn, and I was on the piano just kinda, you know how the blues go, you just kinda *(hums a blues tune)*, and he's going —

ACTOR 3/ED BACON *(impatient, snapping his fingers)*: You know, liven it up, liven it up, it's too *sad*!

ACTOR 8/SAMARIA "COOKIE" MITCHUM: And I said "I'm not going to *liven* up that song! *(laugh)* I don't play it like that. *(laughing)* I wanted to go *(singing, bluesy)* "Aaaaahaa-mazziiiiing graace," you know. And he wanted—

ACTOR 3/ED BACON *(In a martial rhythm—beautiful, but fast)*: A-*maz*-ing *Grace* how *sweet* the *sound* that *saved* a *wretch* like *me*! I *once* was *lost*—

ACTOR 8/SAMARIA "COOKIE" MITCHUM: I said "wait a minute!!" *(laughing, hitting him playfully)* That's not "Amazing Grace"!

ACTOR 3/ED BACON *(good natured)*: That's *my* amazing grace.

ACTOR 8/SAMARIA "COOKIE" MITCHUM: I said "noooo"! I said "nooo, that ain't the way that goes!" I wanted him to put some feeling into it. I had to teach him how, you know you get the *soul* out of a song. *(laughing)*

ACTOR 3/ED BACON: So it was as if she were my, um, gospel music seminar professor.

ACTOR 8/SAMARIA "COOKIE" MITCHUM: You know, but it *really* didn't make a difference, because after the singing was over, it was just as if you hadn't done anything. I mean, I think it did something for Dean Hendricks, and it may have done something for some—like Ed Bacon—he just acted like one of us. You know, you didn't see black and white when you saw Ed. But the *majority* of the whites just considered that a form of entertainment. I think they sincerely felt that God created a world to be segregated. They said "well, it's ok for you to be over here; we're all God's children. But you're supposed to remain here, and I'm supposed to remain here. He does not intend for us to be together."

(ED bends over COOKIE, looking with interest at her song-book.)

THE CHURCH CRUCIFIED

ACTOR 6: From *Ashes for Breakfast* by Tommy Holmes:

ACTOR 4: Two Mercer Negro students first broke the color barrier of Tatnall Square Baptist Church at the edge of Mercer's campus on June 26, 1966 at the 11 am service.

ACTOR 1/TOMMY HOLMES: I shook hands with the two Negro students and welcomed them to our church.

ACTOR 4: The church voted later that summer *not* to seat Negroes at its worship services.

ACTOR 1/TOMMY HOLMES *(Speaking from a pulpit)*: I cannot be a party to denying any person the right to enter God's house and worship. . . My conscience belongs to God, and a thousand votes by the church would not bind it.

ACTOR 6: When the pastor and his two assistants had continued to preach and to declare that the house of God should be open to all persons, the deacons recommended to the church that pastoral services of the three be terminated.

ACTOR 7: Words of these developments came to Sam Oni in California where he had spent the summer in study.

ACTOR 9/SAM ONI: I arrived in California, and it was a daily celebration. I mean, I used to pinch myself and say "hey, what is the matter with you—you're laughing again. You're smiling spontaneously again." I had actually made up my mind that I won't be returning to Mercer.

And then one day I'm walking into the international house, and the news in the vending machine at the entrance—the *Berkeley Gazette*—with a column by Ralph McGill. The headline was "Baptist Pastor to be Fired." So I started reading it: "Tatnall Square Baptist Church, situated on Mercer University Campus. . .The congregation has decided to fire the pastor, Tommy Holmes, for daring to invite in some black students." Ohhhh I read that and I was *livid!* I decided that now there's no doubt in my mind that I would be returning to Mercer. I had *one* more battle to fight.

So I came back. And I remember that Sunday so vividly. I put on my coat and tie and headed out, and as I walked up the steps, the ushers promptly stiffened and blocked my way. And I tried to explain to them, you know, that I wanted to come because there was something about to happen in the church that I thought would be inimical to the faith, and to God's work.

ACTOR 5: Oni was then seized by two deacons of the church. One applied a headlock on him, and the other dragged him down the steps.

ACTOR 1/TOMMY HOLMES: These were the happenings *outside* of the church on the corner of the Baptist university campus the morning of September 25, 1966. They were matched by what occurred inside, which Oni was not able to stop.

ACTOR 10: The congregation voted 250 to 189 to oust their three ministers.

ACTOR 5: Ralph McGill in an editorial on September 2 in the *Atlanta Constitution*:

ACTOR 3: "If this were not so ineffably sad it would be hysterically funny."

ACTOR 5: From the *Mercer Cluster*:

ACTOR 4: "If God is dead, it's churches like Tattnall Square that killed him"

ACTOR 1/TOMMY HOLMES: Here indeed was the church, crucified and bleeding.

(The following should chaotically run into each other, with actors beginning lines simultaneously or interrupting the speaker before them on the italicized sections. The stage should be segregated.)

ACTOR 2: Good race relations have existed in this community *for the last 10 or 15 years—*

ACTOR 5: The basic requirement God set up for his "holy" people *was racial segregation—*

ACTOR 3: Neither shall thou make *marriages with them—*

ACTOR 4: Jesus taught inequality *among men—*

ACTOR 2: Get that nigger out of *our neighborhood—*

ACTOR 6: Thy daughter thou shalt not give unto *his son—*

ACTOR 3: Jesus taught *discerning love—*

ACTOR 2: I suggest they wear *black stars—*

ACTOR 5: nor his daughter shalt thou take unto *thy son*—

ACTOR 3: Sam, do you *know the Lord?*

ACTOR 1: Don't you like that, holding a white *woman's hand?*

ACTOR 4: I predict that in the immediate future we will be *ruled by "darkies"*—

ACTOR 2: mixed weak-minded *generation*—

ACTOR 5: Sam, do you *know the Lord?*

ACTOR 3: Integration is of the *devil*—

ACTOR 6: an unwritten *law*—

ACTORS 2 AND 3: Do you know *the Lord?*

ACTOR 3: most horrible crime against the *Laws of God*—

ACTOR 2: anyone who teaches integration is *bound for Hell*—

ACTORS 1, 3 AND 6: Do you know the Lord?

ACTOR 6: A lot of Good Baptists will leave the church when it is integrated—

ACTOR 7: They haven't left yet.

ACTOR 1: Sinner!

ACTOR 4: Liberal!

ACTOR 3: Communist!

ACTOR 2: Faggot!

ACTOR 5: Race-mixer!

ACTOR 3: Nigger-lover!

ACTOR 9: I'm a nobody.

ACTOR 10: I'm a nobody

ACTOR 8: I'm a nobody.

ACTOR 7: I'm a nobody.

ACTOR 10: I came from the woods.

ACTOR 8: I have no village.

ACTOR 9: I have no degrees.

ACTOR 7: I speak. Who do I speak for?

ACTOR 10: Yahweh.

ACTOR 1: Race-mixer!

ACTOR 5: Trouble-maker!

ACTOR 3: Rabble-rouser!

ACTOR 9: Combustible!

ACTORS 3 & 4: Burn!

ACTOR 8: Combustible!

ACTORS 2 & 6: Burn!

ACTORS 7-10: Combustible

ACTORS 2, 5, 6: Burn!

ACTORS 1, 3, 4: Burn!

ACTORS 1-6 *(shouting)*: BURN!

ED BACON'S VISION

(ED BACON and SAMARIA "COOKIE" MITCHUM are sitting together at the piano. Actors are standing casually or reclining. In the following, the last few words ought to be shared with the next narrator, each voice partaking in the italicized voice of the other, mingling with the voice of the other. The stage should be completely integrated, with at least a few actors in physical contact with each other. The following should be spoken slowly, luxuriantly—the opposite in feeling of the previous scene.)

ACTOR 3/ED BACON: I was six. I was playing alone in this pine grove that was next to the Baptist church *where my father was pastor,*

ACTOR 8: *where my father was pastor,* and um, I don't remember what *time of year it was,*

ACTOR 1: *time of year it was,* it was warm and I— I just remember all the sensations of *the warmth and the light*

ACTOR 6: *the warmth and the light,* and also the smell of the pine needles kind of *baking in the sun*

ACTOR 7: *baking in the sun,* and everything was wonderful, *everything was pleasant*

ACTOR 4: *everything was pleasant,* and all of a sudden I had an *experience*

ACTOR 10: *experience* in which I felt *enveloped*

ACTOR 5: *enveloped* by light and love, *acceptance*

ACTOR 9: *acceptance,* and at the same time felt that I was *the most special*

ACTOR 2: *the most special* and the most beloved of God's creatures, and that *everyone else was also*

ACTOR 1: *everyone else was also.* It was just pure joy, just *pure joy*

ACTOR 8: *pure joy*—I was amazed at how joyful I felt, how *happy I felt*

ACTOR 3/ED BACON: *happy I felt.* I just can't explain that: it was a deep, undisputed, unshakeable connection with God *and*—

ACTORS 3, 4, 8, 9: with all of creation

ACTOR 3: and knowing the relationship between God and creation—that it was total love and acceptance.

ACTOR 8/COOKIE: For someone to have the divine energy in one—

ACTOR 1: which is love,

ACTOR 7: which is the spirit,

ACTOR 9: which is the breath of God—

ACTOR 3/ED BACON: is to be a person who can dream—

ACTORS 3/ED BACON AND 8/SAMARIA "COOKIE" MITCHUM: and have visions.

(The following is spoken softly, overlapping)

ACTOR 8: When you start a fire—

ACTOR 9: When you start a fire—

ACTOR 1: When you start a fire—

ACTOR 4: When you start a fire—

ACTOR 8: You want it to burn—

(Whispers.)

ACTOR 1: Burn—

ACTOR 5: Burn—

ACTOR 8: Burn—

ACTOR 9: Burn—

ACTOR 10: Burn.

Closure

ACTOR 3/HARRIS MOBLEY: The ending? (*laughing*) Oh I'd leave the ending provocative. After all, some helluva good teachers, including that Jew-boy from Nazareth, *(laughing)* I'll tell you buddy, They never give answers! Oh, I wouldn't *dare* answer such a problem *(laughing)* of why a bunch of cotton-picking, holy-roller Baptists *(laughs)* shouted Jesus for a century and a half from Penfield to Macon and then denied any African Americans to attend the place! The questions are the things that will survive. The answers will become shelf-worn. Oh, it has to be provocative. *(laughing)* Oh me. Speak Hebrew. And if people don't understand, that's good!

ACTOR 1/MAC BRYAN: Are you going to admit that integration is a failure? Not just at Mercer but throughout the land? I see it. As do you. Blacks gathering at one place on campus, whites at another. In the cafeteria, social events, concert hall, athletic events. Black fraternities and sororities, white fraternities and sororities. How many white students attend black history month functions? Or enroll in black studies? There is no such thing as closure. Without genuine repentance on the part of the offending party there can be no real reconciliation. Where are the evidences of repentance at Mercer or in Macon?

ACTOR 9/GARY JOHNSON *(Mercer graduate and first full-time African American professor)*: You can't have a neat ending. The sixties here, it was a messy thing. Life is not that neat. I'm not sure you can capture that kind of intensity and anger and the thing that was sort of gnawing at you inside. *(pause)* Now I haven't admitted this before, but I would never do this again if I knew what I know now. I've not even admitted that to Joe—we always talk about it in very positive terms: that it was a good experience, a good thing, but *(pause)* no. Just, just, *(exhales)* ah you know, it's hard to say what you— I guess the question is: what did we do it *for*?

ACTOR 7/CATHERINE MEEKS, *(first full-time African American woman professor)*: At the very heart of being somebody who stands up for social justice is some understanding that just because you might be free, that's not good enough until everybody is free. When you can drive up and down streets in Macon, Georgia and not see the deadness that you see—I mean it's the twenty-first century, and we're still segregated in Macon.

ACTOR 9/SAM ONI: Jesus said "as much as you didn't recognize my divinity in these other brothers and sisters of mine"—to that extent you haven't done it for me. Therefore it's almost an abomination for me to treat a person as less than something divine. Once you recognize the divine in you and me—and you behave consistent with that knowledge—you're *liberated*! Your brother's liberated! Your sister's liberated! *(smiling)* And that then becomes a dance.

ACTOR 3: To some, any dissent from their creed becomes an expressed disbelief in God and man. To them, a change of interpretation, instead of indicating a growth, becomes a direct attempt to undermine the fundamentals of religion. *(Optimistic, excited)* Man's growth is continuous. Only the methods of man harden like shells, and must be broken by every succeeding age. We live in a new age and all our paths are new paths. We move on the crest of a world-change. So rapid is the advance that few realize what a day, a year, a decade may bring forth in national and racial life.

ACTOR 10 *(a sudden change of mood—sad, serious, a challenge)*: That was from *The Mercerian, 1900.*

ACTOR 7/CATHERINE MEEKS: We want closure. And there can be no closure until everybody's liberated. Look around. We still have a long way to go.

(SAMARIA "COOKIE" MITCHUM begins to sing "Amazing Grace." She carries a candle. ED BACON joins in immediately, and she lights his candle. He is joined by SAM ONI, who lights MAC BRYAN's

candle. The cast joins in and finishes the first verse of the song. A pause.)

ACTOR 3: When you start a fire—

ACTOR 8: —you want it to burn.

(The four lean forward and blow their candles out, letting the smoke rise. If using projection, the last image on the screen is of children, African American and white, at Koinonia in 1950. The picture should linger for a few moments in silence. A moment of possibility, lost.)

THE END

TIME LINE

1942: Clarence Jordan co-founds Koinonia farms, an integrated, pacifist commune in Americus, Georgia.

1948: Mac Bryan and Harold McManus, both graduates of Yale Divinity School, are hired by Mercer's Christianity Department. Mac Bryan founds "Little Koinonia" on Mercer's campus and the first copies of *Combustible/Burn* are distributed.

1950: Lawrence Hardy refuses to ride in the front of the bus and breaks Macon's laws by inviting his African American students to play in Tatnall Square Park. Clarence Jordan and his family are excommunicated from Rehobath Southern Baptist Church for bringing a man from India to worship services and for advocating the church's desegregation.

1952: Einar Michaelson is fired from his job at the Georgia Baptist Junior College for publicly advocating desegregation in churches. Harris Mobley has his "spiritual experience" on Route 17 and returns to school.

1953: Mac Bryan's Christian Ethics class votes an African American man into their classroom. The administration later tells the man that he must wait outside the class.

1954: Clifford York and Richard Scott are arrested for having a barbecue together in Clifford's backyard. Clifford York and Mary Wilder graduate.

The Brown vs. Board of Education Supreme Court Decision rules that the segregation of public schools solely on the basis of race is unconstitutional because it deprives children of the minority group equal educational opportunities. "We conclude, unanimously," Justice Earl Warren wrote for the court, "that in the field of public education the doctrine of 'separate but equal' has no place. Separate educational facilities are inherently unequal."

1955: Harris Mobley and Joe Hendricks graduate from Mercer. Mobley later studies with Mac Bryan at Wake Forest University's Divinity School.

The Montgomery Bus Boycott is launched after Rosa Parks gets arrested for refusing to give up her seat on a bus for a white passenger. A year later, the buses desegregate.

1956: Mac Bryan leaves Mercer University after he is relieved from summer teaching duties because of his discussions of Martin Luther King, Jr. Bob Otto is hired to fill his position. Local businesses begin the boycott of Koinonia products; the produce stand is bombed and destroyed; and shots are fired into Koinonia homes from the highway. Carolyn Martin and Nancy Holloway graduate from Mercer.

Dwight D. Eisenhower is reelected as President. The Supreme Court rules on bus desegregation, outlawing segregation on public transportation.

1957: A Grand Jury investigates Koinonia farms. White citizens ask Clarence Jordan to leave the county. After the violence against Koinonia, only five to eight people remain on the farm. Koinonia's mail-order pecan business begins with the slogan: "help ship the nuts out of Georgia."

The Southern Christian Leadership Conference is founded with Martin Luther King as the first president. Dwight Eisenhower calls in 1,000 paratroopers to escort nine African American students into an all white Little Rock High School in Arkansas.

1959: Harris Mobley arrives in Africa and is met by Mac Bryan. Mobley later meets Sam Oni, recently thrown out of a secondary school for leading a student protest. Mobley and his wife Vivian help pay for Oni's remaining high school education. Joe Hendricks returns to Mercer, first as Director of Religious Activities and then as Dean of Men.

1960: Rufus Harris becomes Mercer's President.

Sit-ins begin at lunch counters all over the south, including Macon. The Student Non-Violent Coordinating Committee is founded. John F. Kennedy is elected as President.

1961: After a Federal Court order issued by Mercer graduate Judge William Augustus Bootle, African American students Charlene Hunter and Hamilton Holmes are admitted to the University of Georgia.

1962: Rufus Harris publicly advocates Mercer's integration and sets up a committee, headed by Walter Moore, to study its eventual implementation. Sam Oni applies to Mercer University.

University of Mississippi is compelled by a Federal Court to desegregate by admitting James Meredith, its first African American student. Within days, students at Ole Miss riot, killing two and injuring many.

1963: Harris Mobley returns to Mercer to give his chapel speech. Sam Oni, along with Bennie Stephens and Cecil Dewberry, are admitted to Mercer University, making it the first Georgia university to voluntarily desegregate. Don Baxter volunteers to be Oni's roommate. Vineville Baptist Church, under the guidance of Walter Moore, accepts Sam Oni as a member, becoming the first Baptist church in Georgia to desegregate its membership. Three years after the Supreme Court ruling on bus desegregation, Macon's bus system is desegregated after a successful boycott.

Civil rights activists are beaten and hosed at the Birmingham march. Martin Luther King is arrested and writes "Letter from Birmingham Jail." President John F. Kennedy is assassinated. Medgar Evers, NAACP leader, is murdered in Mississippi. 250,000 people attend the March on Washington, where Martin Luther King Jr. gives his "I Have a Dream" speech on the steps of the Lincoln Memorial. Four African American girls attending Sunday School are killed in a bombing of a Baptist church active in Birmingham's civil rights movement.

1964: Macon begins public school desegregation, a process that will not be complete until the 1970's, twenty years after the Brown vs. Board of Education decision. Samaria "Cookie" Mitchum joins six other African American students to enroll at a white high school.

Lyndon Johnson is elected President. Johnson signs the Civil Rights Act Bill, which makes discrimination in the workplace and segregation in public facilities illegal. Three civil rights activists—Andrew Goodman, Michael Schwerner, and James Cheney—are murdered while registering African American voters in Mississippi.

1965: Samaria "Cookie" Mitchum enrolls at Mercer.

Lyndon Johnson signs the Voting Rights Act. Malcolm X is assassinated.

1966: Tatnall Square Baptist Church, located on the edge of Mercer's campus, votes to fire its minister, Tommy Holmes, after he allows two of Mercer's African American Upward Bound students to worship. Sam Oni returns from California to protest. Joe Hendricks and Johnny Mitchell recruit the largest class of African American students yet at Mercer.

1967: Sam Oni and Bennie Stephens graduate. Ed Bacon and Samaria "Cookie" Mitchum sing together in Sunday gatherings arranged by Joe Hendricks and his sister, Jean.

1968: Betty J. Walker becomes the first African American woman to graduate from Mercer.

Martin Luther King Jr. is assassinated and violence breaks out in more than a hundred cities. President Lyndon Johnson signs the Civil Rights act, which makes discrimination in the sale, rental and financing of housing illegal.

1969: Samaria "Cookie" Mitchum graduates. Clarence Jordan dies at 57 while writing a sermon to be delivered at Mercer. The undertaker refuses to accept his body. Millard Fuller, his protege, delivers Jordan's unfinished sermon at Mercer. Fuller forms Habitat for Humanity in partnership with Koinonia farms. Both Habitat for Humanity and Koinonia farms are still thriving today (their websites are www.koinoniapartners.org and www.habitat.org).

1970: Gary Johnson, Lydia Dumas, Ernestine Cole, Maureen Walker graduate.

Designed in 12/14 Minion
by Marc A. Jolley
at Mercer University Press
Printed and bound by McNaughton & Gunn, Inc.
Cover design by Jim Burt, Burt & Burt Studio

Mercer University Press
MMII
www.mupress.org